"With *Faith in the Shadows*, Aust[...]
and into the limelight of leading
pastor-theologians. This book i[...]
struggles with issues of Christian raith [...]
and confused world. The line between hardcore fundamen[...]
insipid theological liberalism is a fine one these days; most people fall
to one side or the other. Fischer helpfully points out the path between
and beyond them."
Roger E. Olson, Foy Valentine Professor of Christian Theology and
Ethics, George W. Truett Theological Seminary, Baylor University

"'But some doubted' is one of the most jarring expressions in the entire
Bible. After hearing Jesus, after watching Jesus, after knowing Jesus up
close and personal, after his crucifixion and the apocalyptic moment
of his resurrection, some of the disciples still doubted. How could that
be? How could those who were so close to Jesus doubt anything about
him? That's why Austin Fischer wrote this book, and it's a book for
that kind of doubter: the one who knows about Jesus and has experienced Jesus, but still wonders—who still finds gaps instead of connec-
tions, who still limps after having run with the saints. In his deceptively
perceptive exploration, Fischer focuses on the 'hypocrisy of certainty'—
that confidence where none should be had. Honesty demands we admit
our doubts; honesty is what this book is about."
Scot McKnight, Julius R. Mantey Professor of New Testament,
Northern Seminary

"For those of you acquainted with pain and doubt, Austin is definitely
the pastor you need in your life! And for those of you who pretend
so hard that you have no pain and doubt, Austin is definitely the pastor
you need in your life! I live in both categories regularly, so I'm glad I
got to feast on his wisdom for a few hundred pages while I read *Faith
in the Shadows*. Austin gave me permission to think, to cry, and to be.
And for that I am extremely grateful. Now is your turn to enjoy this
beautiful collection of stories and invitations, reminders and experiences, Jesus and us. Enjoy."
Carlos A. Rodríguez, pastor and founder of The Happy NPO,
author of *Drop the Stones*

FAITH
IN THE
SHADOWS

FINDING CHRIST
in the
MIDST OF DOUBT

AUSTIN FISCHER

FOREWORD BY BRIAN ZAHND

IVP Books

An imprint of InterVarsity Press
Downers Grove, Illinois

InterVarsity Press
P.O. Box 1400, Downers Grove, IL 60515-1426
ivpress.com
email@ivpress.com

InterVarsity Press® *is the book-publishing division of InterVarsity Christian Fellowship/USA*®, *a movement of students and faculty active on campus at hundreds of universities, colleges, and schools of nursing in the United States of America, and a member movement of the International Fellowship of Evangelical Students. For information about local and regional activities, visit intervarsity.org.*

All Scripture quotations, unless otherwise indicated, are taken from the New American Standard Bible®, *copyright 1960, 1962, 1963, 1968, 1971, 1972, 1973, 1975, 1977, 1995 by The Lockman Foundation. Used by permission.*

While any stories in this book are true, some names and identifying information may have been changed to protect the privacy of individuals.

Cover design: David Fassett
Interior design: Daniel van Loon

ISBN 978-0-8308-4543-9 (print)
ISBN 978-0-8308-7402-6 (digital)

Printed in the United States of America ♾

Library of Congress Cataloging-in-Publication Data
Names: Fischer, Austin, 1985- author.
Title: Faith in the shadows : finding Christ in the midst of doubt / Austin Fischer.
Description: Downers Grove : InterVarsity Press, 2018. | Includes
  bibliographical references.
Identifiers: LCCN 2018017717 (print) | LCCN 2018026181 (ebook) |
  ISBN 9780830874026 (eBook) | ISBN 9780830845439 (pbk. : alk. paper)
Subjects: LCSH: Faith.
Classification: LCC BT771.3 (ebook) | LCC BT771.3 .F57 2018 (print) |
  DDC 234/.23—dc23
LC record available at https://lccn.loc.gov/2018017717

P 25 24 23 22 21 20 19 18 17 16 15 14 13 12 11 10 9 8 7 6 5 4 3 2 1

Y 35 34 33 32 31 30 29 28 27 26 25 24 23 22 21 20 19 18

For my boys

In memory of Everett

CONTENTS

FOREWORD

BRIAN ZAHND

few years ago, a pastor of an evangelical-fundamentalist church with whom I'm acquainted announced on the Sunday after Easter that he had become an atheist. He told his stunned congregation that he had been an atheist for a year and a half and that all attempts to revive his faith had failed. So on the Sunday after Easter he publicly left Christianity and moved on with his life—a life with no more Easters.

A few days after his bombshell resignation I met with this now erstwhile pastor. As I listened to his story, it quickly became apparent that he had not so much lost his faith in Christianity as he had lost his credulity for fundamentalism. Sadly, he had been formed in a tradition where Christianity and fundamentalism were so tightly bound together that he could not make a distinction between them.

For this fundamentalist pastor, if the Bible wasn't literally, historically, and scientifically factual in a biblicist-empiricist sense, then Christianity was a falsity he had to reject. When his fundamentalist house of cards collapsed, it took his Christian faith down with it. In one remarkable leap of faith, a fundamentalist became a newly minted atheist. I did my best to explain to him that he had made the modern mistake of confusing historical Christian faith with early twentieth-century fundamentalism, but by then the damage was done, and it appears his faith has suffered a fatal blow.

This story I've briefly related is true, but it's also a postmodern parable. By misinterpreting the Enlightenment and the corresponding rise of empiricism as an existential threat to Christian faith, many frightened Christians sequestered themselves in panic rooms of certitude. Unfortunately, this kind of darkness breeds monsters. Most doubts—like most monsters—are not that scary in the daylight. Most Christians can deal with inevitable doubts as long as there is room for doubt. But when a system is enforced that leaves no room for doubt, benign uncertainties can mutate into faith-destroying monsters. When doubts are locked away in a closet of secrecy they can grow into formidable ogres.

As a pastor I've seen it happen. I've seen fear-based Christian parents place their children in fundamentalist Christian schools for the sole purpose of shielding little Johnny from the "lies of secular science," only to see Johnny become an atheist before he's out of high school. When you force Johnny to choose between fundamentalist certitude and peer-reviewed science, Johnny may not always be persuaded by pseudo-apologetics from fundamentalist answer men like Ken Ham. I've seen it happen.

I've seen too many Christians lose battles they never needed to fight. Like Don Quixote they imagine harmless windmills as threatening giants and fight a needless battle, only to have the windmill-imagined-as-giant win. The culture wars have created these kinds of quixotic crusades—and sometimes the tragic outcome is pastors announcing their atheism on the Sunday after Easter.

These days I have a simple mission statement: to help make Christianity possible for my grandchildren and their generation. I want my seven grandchildren (all under the age of eight) to be able to celebrate Easter for a lifetime. So if my grandchildren are to be able to embrace Easter with any kind of authentic faith when they're adults, I cannot afford to ignore their inevitable doubts or try to strong-arm them into unquestioning certitude. In our secular age that is a formula for atheism. Instead I will do my best to nurture my grandchildren in the rich soil of historic Christian faith—a faith that in its healthiest forms has always been comfortable with mystery and nuance, metaphor and allegory, candid questions and honest doubt. Because in the end, Christianity has suffered more casualties from faux faith than from honest doubt.

In seeking to pass on Christian faith to my grandchildren I am more interested in presenting them with a beautiful mystery than a collection of iron-clad certitudes. If Jesus is presented as as beautiful and mysterious as we find him in the Gospels, I'm willing to trust in that beauty to win hearts. I've heard it said that no one ever became a Christian because they lost an argument. I suspect that's true. I also suspect far more people than we imagine have become converts to Christianity for the simple reason that they were charmed by the beauty of Christ. I would much rather ground Christian faith on the beauty of Christ than on biblical literalism. Biblical literalism can be debunked by a college freshman, but the beauty of Christ can withstand every attack Nietzsche can muster. If I'm hedging my bets on the survival of Christian faith as we hurdle into a secular age, it's because the King of Hearts is still so beautiful. I'm willing to bet my grandchildren's faith on the beauty of Christ.

And in my mission to help make Christianity possible for the generations that follow, I have a trusted and gifted ally in Austin Fischer. *Faith in the Shadows* is the kind of book that can give faith the space to flourish—not by beating back doubt through dogmatic argument, but by taking the terror out of doubt by exposing it to the sunlight of honest reflection. Fischer's book bears the subtitle *Finding Christ in the Midst of Doubt*. I like that. When we succumb to the dualism of Christ versus Doubt locked in a battle to the death, we are taking an unnecessary risk. It's enough to find the beauty of Christ in the dark night of doubt. I have sufficient faith to believe I don't have to dispel every doubt with a clever argument; it's enough to allow the beauty of Christ to shine in the midst of doubt.

Fischer writes with a wonderful combination of keen intellect and unflinching honesty. He hits all the necessary topics, from fundamentalism to theodicy, while drawing on our best Christian thinkers, from Fyodor Dostoyevsky to David Bentley Hart. But what Fischer does best is invite the reader into his own struggles with doubt, showing how he has been able to find Christ even in the midst of doubt. Ultimately, the hero of Fischer's book is not the brilliant Christian apologists (though we appreciate their fruitful labors) but the beauty of Christ's love that is the only credible answer to interrogations of doubt. As Fischer says, "Faith is not the absence of doubt. Faith is the presence of love."

My only regret about *Faith in the Shadows* is that it wasn't written in time to be read by a Missouri pastor struggling all alone with growing doubts. If it had, perhaps his faith could have survived to celebrate another Easter.

*R*embrandt's *The Return of the Prodigal Son* hangs on a wall in my office, and each day I sit opposite it and meditate on it. This ritual will sound familiar to those acquainted with the work of Henri Nouwen because in *The Return of the Prodigal Son*, Nouwen recounts his journey with this painting: a window into the mysterious, redemptive way of God in the world. Art historian H. W. Janson calls it "a moment stretching into eternity." I agree.

When I started following Christ, I saw myself in the prodigal, dressed in rags and tattered sandals, falling on my knees and into the arms of mercy, hoping those arms would wrap me up and not push me away. And they did, because mercy is real.

Time passed and I got my act together. I rose from my knees. I walked with a swagger instead of a limp. And somewhere along the way I forget what it's like to be barefoot and living on a prayer. I became the older brother.

He stands off to the side, partly in the shadows, disappointed as he watches his father embrace the prodigal. His brow is not furrowed. His hands are not thrown up. He isn't outraged—he's mellow, reposed, unmoved. The scene unfolding in front of him is too sentimental and unseemly. His prodigal brother doesn't deserve this welcome, and his father should have more dignity. Hiking up his robe to run out and greet this son-turned-beggar? Embracing him unreservedly? Important people do not act this way. His father should know better; his brother deserves worse.

More time passed, and as I let the painting do its proper work, my eyes were drawn, again and again, to one place in particular: the father's hands. Though not the literal center of the painting, they hold the painting together. They have gravity. Our eyes wander but always return to those hands. It's strange that something so human could point to something so divine; or maybe it isn't.

Those hands rest on the shoulders of the prodigal. They hold him close. They seem gentle but firm. They will not squeeze him into submission, but they will never let him go. Indeed, the two hands are very different. As many commentators have pointed out, one is masculine and one is feminine. The left hand is thick and muscular; the right hand is elegant and graceful. A father's hand and a mother's hand? That was Nouwen's guess.

These hands hold the painting together and perhaps they hold everything together. Perhaps the *what* and *why* of everything—from laughter to cancer to stars—is found in those gentle, firm hands. And perhaps we have no greater purpose than *to be* those hands. As Nouwen writes, "The return to the Father is ultimately the challenge to become the Father." Saint Paul concurs: "Therefore, we are ambassadors for Christ, as though God were making an appeal through us; we beg you on behalf of Christ, be reconciled to God" (2 Corinthians 5:20). We walk the world as the reconciliation of God, welcoming prodigal creation back into the arms of its maker. The story of the universe hangs in a print of a painting on a wall in my office, and this brings me to the woman in the shadows. I did not see her at first.

In seminary, I was assigned Nouwen's book, and on the first day of class, our professor had us look at the picture of Rembrandt's painting on the front cover. Due to the poor resolution, only five figures were visible: the father, the prodigal, the older brother, and an unidentified man and woman. Three years later, I opened the box containing my recently purchased (and high quality) print, and for the first time, I saw the sixth figure.

There she was, up in the far left corner—tucked away in the shadows, the faintest light on her face. She is watching the father and prodigal embrace, but she is also watching the people who are watching the embrace—the older brother and the unidentified man and woman. Shrouded in darkness, she has one foot in the scene and one foot out. One wonders both what she sees and how she feels about what she sees. These are her secrets, and they are not disclosed cheaply. If you want to see what she sees, you must stand where she stands: on the fringes.

I AM A PASTOR

I am a pastor. I did not grow up wanting to be a pastor. I wanted to be a basketball player. From the time I could walk, there was a basketball hoop set up in the living room and we (my father, my little brother, and I) raced up and down the "court" as my mother looked on in adoration, amusement, and anxiety. Many decorative trinkets were broken over the years, but my mother loved her boys and always let the game go on.

But eventually every Peter Pan has to grow up, so, realizing I might need a vocational backup plan should my basketball dreams fail, I decided I could settle for becoming a lawyer. My parents assured me this was a good idea because someone as argumentative as I am might as well get paid handsomely for it. So it was settled—I would be a lawyer.

And yet here I am, a pastor, because I followed a breadcrumb trail that led me to the feet of a crucified God and a mystery I will spend the rest of my life making sense of because it continues to make sense of me. That is a story for another day, but suffice to say, I was not blinded on the road to Damascus. In fact, I often feel like I have more in common with Paul's bewildered companions than with Paul. I hear the voice he hears but cannot always see what he sees. There are wonders I have not been made privy to, and sometimes, even as a pastor and minister of light, I am left on the outside looking in—one foot in and one foot out.

Indeed I once sat staring at Rembrandt's painting and found, to my surprise, the center of gravity had changed. I did not look at the father's hands or the prodigal's mangy scalp or the older brother's downward gaze—I looked at the woman in the shadows. I could not stop looking at the woman in the shadows. And suddenly I found myself standing in the shadows with her, seeing the scene from behind her eyes, sharing her secrets. Better yet, I realized that I had been standing in the shadows with her for a while, that, in a certain sense, I have always stood in the shadows with her. And not wanting my faith to stay stuck in the shadows forever, I started a slow journey into the light.

WORSHIPING DOUBTERS

I love being a pastor and am called to be a pastor, but at times, doubt comes more naturally for me than faith. When a child dies, I don't see a hidden joy and design behind the tragedy; I see nonsense. I don't feel divinely comforted; I feel rage. So if you need your pastor to make it all make sense, to tie all the suffering nonsense up with a tidy bow, then I will disappoint you.

There are both a blessing and a curse here. The curse is that many things I've been told are "supposed" to come naturally for pastors do not come naturally for me. The blessing is that my situation has forced me to develop habits that can shape and sustain me as I live a life in service to a faith that does not always come naturally. What my faith lacks in ease it makes up for in grit, which is just as well because easy faith comes with its own set of problems: "Just as an athlete with natural gifts may fail to develop the fundamental skills necessary to play his or her sport after the talent fades, so people naturally disposed to faith may fail to develop the skills necessary to sustain them for a lifetime." My bags are packed for the long haul. I hope yours are too. Because at some point in your life, I suspect you too might find yourself on the fringes of faith, and as you stand there in the shadows you will need grit. You will also need to know you are not alone and many stand with you.

When we walk down the long hallway of Christian faith, we find that many of our saints also had an inner skeptic. Think of Sarah, laughing at God's promise to give her and Abraham a son in their advanced age. Think of Moses, the man who would argue with a burning and talking bush, insisting God had the wrong guy. Think of the despair in the lament psalms. Think of the apostles scoffing at the prospects of an empty tomb—the great apostles, first skeptics of the resurrection! Their skepticism has something to teach us, which leads us to the story of the Great Commission.

Jesus, newly risen, gathers his apostles and sends them out into the nations, making disciples and baptizing in the name of the Father, Son, and Holy Spirit. But few recall what precedes this. The eleven apostles journey to a mountain in Galilee. They've been told Jesus will meet them there. They reach the top and there he is—the resurrected Christ! And what happens next is so incredibly strange: "When they saw him, they worshiped him; but some doubted" (Matthew 28:17 NIV).

Wait. How could someone stand on top of a mountain, stare into the eyes of the resurrected Christ, and still doubt? How is that possible? This is a haunting question, to be sure, but it invites another question:

Why do most of us not know this story?

Given how deeply so many struggle with skepticism and doubt, how is it possible the church has not told us this story over and over? How is it possible so many people think their doubts disqualify them from faith when some of the apostles looked into the eyes of the resurrected Christ and still doubted?

Around a third of people who leave faith do so because of skepticism and doubt. Over a third of young adult Christians feel they cannot ask their most pressing questions in church. And over a third of young adult Christians feel Christians are too confident they have all the answers. Add these numbers and something becomes very clear and very sad. Doubt makes people abandon faith, but people don't abandon faith because they have doubts. People abandon faith because they think they're not allowed to have doubts. People abandon faith because, intentionally or unintentionally, they've been forced into an impossible, unbiblical, binary choice: you can have Jesus or you can have doubts, but you cannot have both.

So what will it be? Jesus or our doubts?

Thanks be to God, this is not a decision we have to make, and this brings us back to that mountain where the risen Christ stands with the eleven apostles.

Translating the Bible into English can be a bit tricky at times, and Matthew 28:17 is one of those times. Some difficult interpretive decisions have to be made in translation, and many translations make it sound as if some of the disciples are worshiping and some are doubting—as if ten are worshiping and one is doubting (we're looking at you, Thomas). But a strong argument can be made, on grammatical and narrative grounds, that it is best translated, "When they saw him, they worshiped him, but were not sure."

In other words, it's not that some worship while some doubt—it's that all worship *and* all doubt. They all worship, even though they're uncertain. Two thousand years ago, Jesus gathered a group of worshiping doubters on a mountain, sent them out, and the world was never the same. And this is why no one should ever think they must choose between Jesus and doubt. The church is built on people who lived the contradiction.

WHITE ROSES AND BRIGHT RED LIPSTICK

On three nights in February 1943, three German university students did something simple, courageous, and reckless. Hans Scholl, Alexander Schmorell, and Willi Graf were members of The White Rose, a nonviolent, anti-Nazi resistance group. Over the course of a few months, they anonymously published six different leaflets deploring Nazi tyranny, calling on Germans to rise up and rebel. "We will not be silent. We are your bad conscience. The White Rose will not leave you in peace!"

Slinking through the shadows, they painted anti-Nazi graffiti on the sides of houses along a busy street near the University of Munich. The people of Munich woke up to "Down with Hitler," "Freedom," and crossed-out swastikas defacing their concrete walls. Soon after, they were discovered and beheaded.

Initially, little was made of it all. Their executions incited no rebellion. Many even felt their actions were unpatriotic. But as it often does, time changed things, and The White Rose now stands as a symbol of aggressive compassion and bravery in the face of hatred. They plastered their defiant, hopeful graffiti across a cold, concrete canvas, and though it was little more than an act of amateur vandalism, time has chiseled it into the stone of collective memory. It's amazing what a bit of graffiti can do, and there are potential canvases everywhere.

I knew a lady in a nursing home who always wore bright red lipstick, which struck me as sad and vain. She was very elderly and sickly, and no one visited. Why did she always wear bright red lipstick? One day I walked into her room, and as usual, she immediately reapplied a layer of lipstick. My amused judgment must have shown through because she paused mid-application, looked at me, and said, "Oh, I know it probably seems a bit vain, but the hell with it—I'm dying and it reminds me this isn't the end." And with that, she held her head high and shamelessly returned to application. She died a few months later, and I wept and laughed simultaneously when I walked by her casket and saw her—pale and gaunt but wearing a fresh coat of bright red lipstick. When I walk with people through the valley of the shadow of death, I now tell them the story of her bright red graffiti.

Some people are ashamed of their doubts, and some are proud of them. I have been both and now I try to be neither—I try to be faithful with my doubts. And so what follows is some of my graffiti, my ongoing and never-quite-finished Easter rebellion against the cold canvas of death and doubt.

The church has always been a place for skeptics and saints and skeptical saints. So wherever you find yourself on the continuum between faith and doubt, grab some paint, or bright red lipstick, or whatever you can find, and make a mess. You don't have to be Rembrandt. The walls of the kingdom of God will feature the amateur graffiti of many hope-filled vandals.

CHAPTER TWO

ANTS ON A ROLLERCOASTER

For thousands of years we thought Earth was the center of the universe. We thought the sun and moon and stars revolved around Earth. And we thought Earth was stable and unmoving—a firm island of objectivity amid the swirling sea of the cosmos. It certainly looks and feels that way. But now we know none of this is true.

Now we know that we are tiny ants who live in a tiny corner of a massive planet; a massive planet spinning on its axis at a thousand miles per hour, while orbiting the sun at the center of our solar system at 66,000 miles per hour; a solar system flying around our galaxy at 450,000 miles per hour; a galaxy whirling through the universe at a couple million miles per hour.

Do you ever trip and not know why?

In the deep ocean of space, there is a giant. Visible to the naked eye on a clear night in the southern hemisphere, Eta Carinae might be the biggest star in the galaxy—one hundred times bigger and five million times brighter than the Sun. Fortunately, it is located about 7,500 light years away. But if it were to die in a hypernova explosion, it could release a gamma-ray burst so powerful that a direct hit might trigger a major extinction event, the end of our little ant colony—sobering, isn't it? The death of a giant star—impossibly far away, farther than the mind can possibly imagine—might be the death of humanity. And we cannot do a thing about it.

We thought we were the kings of the cosmos, but now we know we're ants on a rollercoaster. Now we know the universe is a whole lot bigger—and we're a whole lot smaller—than we could have imagined. As astronomer Carl Sagan has said, "We find that we live on an insignificant planet of a humdrum star lost between two spiral arms in the outskirts of a galaxy which is a member of a sparse cluster of galaxies, tucked away in some forgotten corner of a universe in which there are far more galaxies than people." A universe in which there are far more galaxies than people—who would have known?

So we're tiny and we're not in control. That does not mean we're insignificant or doomed to the fixed winds of fate, but as fallen kings of the cosmos living in rapidly changing times, it is likely to make us *feel* insignificant. The times are always changing, but it certainly seems the times are currently changing at a rate never before seen in the history of the world, with no deceleration in sight. David Kinnaman suggests that a "reasonable argument can be made that no generation of Christians has lived through a set of cultural changes so profound and lightning fast." In particular, technology has created, for all intents and purposes, a new world. Click a few buttons and in a few minutes you can learn more about the world than previous generations could have hoped to learn in a lifetime. Former Google CEO Eric Schmidt claims we now create as much new information every two days as all of humanity collectively created from the dawn of civilization up until 2003.

Our ancient ancestors interacted with a small handful of people each day—their family and perhaps the family who lived in the cave down the street. As technology advanced, social circles widened, and now most of us daily interact with hundreds if not thousands of people. Cars, planes, television, radio, phone, internet—because of them we bump into all sorts of different people all the time, and as we've bumped into all these people we've discovered that we disagree about many things, some of which are awfully important.

Think of something you would stake your life on, something you believe so deeply you would die for it. No matter what that something is, someone else is willing to die for her belief that you're wrong about your belief. I suppose this has always been the case, but we're more aware of it now, and it weighs more heavily on us. We *know* we're ants, and there's no turning back, no putting the genie of hyperpluralism back in the bottle:

> Human life in the western world today . . . is characterized by an enormously wide range of incompatible truth claims pertaining to human values, aspirations, norms, morality, and meaning. . . . A hyperpluralism of religious and secular commitments, not any shared or even convergent view about what "we" think is true or right or good, marks the early twenty-first century.

The endless proliferation of truth claims, coupled with our increasing awareness of them, makes the world feel bigger, all the while making us feel smaller. Many people believing many different things does not mean *nothing* is true (that is, pluralism does not necessitate relativism), but as the beliefs pile up into the heavens, we can't help but wonder if anyone (God or gods or whatever) is actually at home up there. Maybe we are just making it up as we go.

I once listened to a podcast where a Christian and Christian turned agnostic talked about faith and doubt. The Christian was a brilliant professional theologian whereas the agnostic was an amateur. Predictably, the Christian won the exchanges—all except one.

The theologian had skillfully laid out his case for God and faith, and the agnostic fellow conceded as much and even intimated he would very much like to be a good prodigal and return to faith. But he also knew there were countless *Christians* (not atheists or Hindus or Muslims) who would not only disagree with the theologian but go so far as to say the Christian theologian wasn't even really a Christian but a heretic. So how was he to worship God when there was so much disagreement about who God really is and what God is really like, even among those who agree God is Holy Trinity—Father, Son, and Spirit? The theologian lacked a decisive response, and I did too. Some questions haunt us, and their ghosts are not easily exorcised.

Like so many, I was in college when I realized I was an ant. The bigness and diversity of the world accosted me. The claims of science and other religions rang in my ears, contrasting voices ricocheted inside my head, the load on my shoulders grew, and my little ant legs buckled. The universe is a heavy thing for an ant to bear.

INNOCENCE LOST

My son loves our family dog. Her name was one of his first words: Piper. So far as he is concerned, there are no dogs—there are just "Pipers." We haven't bothered trying to explain that while Piper is our dog's name, not all dogs are named Piper. She recently nipped him for the first time, and for a few seconds he didn't even think to cry. He was too shocked. He had run up and hugged her hundreds of times. He had pulled on her tail and ears. He had crawled all over her. She was his best friend, and his best friend had just hurt him. His watery eyes told the familiar story of innocence lost.

Life is a journey from innocence to doubt. It can travel in various directions after doubt, but it will always venture from innocence to doubt. We embrace the world with the wide-eyed gusto of a child, the world pummels us, and we hobble away bewildered, wounded, and confused.

From the time I had faith, faith was my friend, though I came to it kicking and screaming. I vividly remember walking down the aisle with my little brother at First Baptist Church in Lufkin, Texas. He was going forward to ask Jesus into his heart and be baptized, and while I had no clue what that meant and no desire to let a homeless carpenter live in my heart, big brothers don't let little brothers finish first in anything, so if baptism was what it took, I was willing to take the plunge. (The commitment runs deep.) But years later, things changed.

I realized I wanted to follow Jesus because Jesus was good and not because my life was bad. "Come follow Jesus because you live a sad, miserable life and will continue to do so; but heaven will be great" was the gospel I heard. It left me moderately intrigued but mostly bored. Fortunately, Jesus didn't preach this gospel, and in time I discovered that, and I found that faith beckoned me into a life of merciful adventure. Faith was my friend, and then one day it nipped me.

I arrived at college with the brazen gait of someone who just doesn't know how much he doesn't know. Ignorance was bliss, and I deflected any and all challenges to my faith with five magic words: "Because the Bible says so." Yes, there are other religions, but the Bible says Christianity is the truth. Yes, we've never seen a dead person walk out of a tomb, walk through walls, and ascend up into the heavens, but the Bible says it happened. Yes, science indicates the earth is very old, but the Bible says it is fairly young.

Those five words worked miraculously, and so long as you don't think about it too much, they're all you need. But I thought about it too much and finally made myself ask the question all my "because the Bible says so" answers had been begging all along: Why do we think we can trust the Bible?

For some this question is easy to answer. Point to fulfilled prophecies and corroborating archaeological finds. Assert the Bible is inerrant and infallible and self-authenticating. Believe Solomon affirmed the First Law of Thermodynamics in Ecclesiastes 1:10 thousands of years before Rudolf Clausius and William Rankine stumbled on it. And to some the logic of all this is, more or less, airtight. I certainly used to agree.

But I've come to believe it's all a good bit more complicated than that. For one thing, some of these answers are highly contestable and, worse, deceptively circular. For example, reasoning that we can trust the Bible because the Bible says we can trust the Bible is not really very reasonable. It's an assertion pretending to be an argument. And this happens a lot when we defend the Bible. We often struggle to answer questions about the Bible because the Bible is what we use to answer most of our questions. It's like taking off your glasses and trying to inspect them but being unable to do so properly because you can't see without your glasses. Speaking along parallel lines about worldviews, N. T. Wright says, "When you are questioned about some or all of your worldview, and you have . . . to take [your worldview] off and look at it in order to see what's going on, you may not be able to examine it very closely because it is itself the thing through which you normally examine everything else."

On top of that, too much is at stake—we can't afford to play fair. Better yet, all is fair in the defense of faith.

Sometimes a mild case of doubt pops up and a good night's sleep will do, but what I was experiencing was far from benign. A potentially terminal skepticism crept through my bones. My doubt was not going anywhere anytime soon.

BLESSED ARE THE BIGFOOT HUNTERS?

It is strange that your eternal well-being would be determined by your ability (or lack thereof) to convince yourself that something is true, but in much popular theology, this is, allegedly, the case. Faith is the absence of doubt, and some biblical passages appear to nod in this direction: "But when you ask, you must believe and not doubt, because the one who doubts is like a wave of the sea, blown and tossed by the wind. That person should not expect to receive anything from the Lord" (James 1:6-7 NIV). Your faith is measured by the degree of certainty with which you hold your beliefs. Certainty equals strong faith. Doubt equals weak faith.

When we think about faith this way, there is only one acceptable response to having doubt: stuff it down, pretend it's not there, push it out of our mind and heart so we can feel certain again because that's what faith is and what God wants from us. It's certainty or bust. There are a number of problems with this response, and the first is that we are humans, and humans cannot be certain about much of anything.

A little lower than God—Psalm 8 says that's what God made us. Whatever that is, that's what we are, but apparently being even just a little lower than God makes a big difference. We are painfully finite creatures who know far less of reality than we could ever comprehend. We peep out into an infinite universe through a pinhole, during a brief space in time, and no matter how long we live and how much we learn, what we don't know will always greatly outweigh what we do know. These are the facts. So whether we stretch our certainty-lusting hands into the heavens or bury our heads in the sand, certainty will always lie beyond our reach.

As a personal anecdote, I've always found that unbelievers are much less offended by the hypocrisy of our morality than they are the hypocrisy of our certainty. Every human, believer or unbeliever, knows what it's like to fail to live up to one's beliefs, to fail to embody one's moral ideals. Moral hypocrisy is a universal experience, so unbelievers can be remarkably understanding of our moral fragility, because they know it too. What unbelievers fail to understand is how we can pretend to be certain of things we obviously cannot be certain of.

In his short but wonderful book *How to Think*, Alan Jacobs reminds us "there's a proper firmness of belief that lies between the extremes of rigidity and flaccidity." Put more simply, we should seek to find a balance between being open-minded and closed-minded. Be too open-minded and it's impossible to live with any settled conviction. Be too closed-minded and it's impossible to live with any integrity because you are dishonest about the narrow horizons of your own knowledge.

I once spoke with an atheist who told me he would love to hear me explain the coherence of Christian faith, but not until I admitted that, while a believer, I was also uncertain about my beliefs. I asked why and he curtly responded, "Because I haven't any time to waste talking about something this important with someone who lacks the decency to own his humanity and admit we are two uncertain human beings trying to make sense of mysteries. I know that I am an uncertain human. Do you?" Sadly, at the time I did not, so our conversation floundered on the shoals of my unacknowledged uncertainty (or humanity).

So while we often think admitting our doubt and uncertainty would damage our witness to the world, I am now convinced it would mostly do the opposite. Owning our uncertainty does not make our faith less credible but more credible since it makes our faith more human and thus more honest. We need not overcome our humanity to have faith. So if we want to better fulfill the Great Commission, we shouldn't pretend we're certain!

The second problem with the notion that faith is somehow tied to certainty is that it makes us do some very strange things, perhaps the strangest being the virtue it makes us make out of the peculiar psychological ruse that is *convincing yourself* something is true.

In a college class about deviant social behavior, I met a man who had convinced himself that Bigfoot was real and one lived among the loblolly pines outside College Station, Texas. I do not think I could convince myself of something quite like this, but I do know what it's like to try to convince myself something is true, and most important, I know there's nothing particularly virtuous about doing so. We criticize people of other faiths when they pronounce the verdict before really sorting through the evidence, failing to have an "open mind." When we exhibit the same psychological behavior, tipping the scales disingenuously in our favor so we can convince ourselves we are right, we call it faith. But the ability to convince ourselves is not a fruit of the Spirit, nor will the Bigfoot hunters be greatest in the kingdom of God.

There is nothing wrong with being simple or gullible, but making an absolute virtue out of crass fideism is unwise. As Voltaire allegedly stated, "Doubt is not a pleasant condition, but certainty is absurd." Trying to convince yourself that you're certain of something you know good and well you cannot possibly be certain of is torturous beyond measure, and any God who would leverage anything of consequence on it is, frankly, not a God worth believing in, much less worshiping. And yet many people go through life thinking the healing of loved ones, the answering of prayers, and eternal destinies hang in the balance as they courageously try to "just believe." It is certainty seeking faith. We convince ourselves because we don't trust God to convince us.

Once at my church, I preached on the absurdity of certainty seeking faith, and afterwards a sage elderly lady asked me about Hebrews 11:1: "Now faith is the assurance of things hoped for, the conviction of things not seen." The verse is just vague enough to be interpreted in a number of ways, so context is key.

Hebrews 11:1 provides us with a nonexhaustive description of what faith is and does before the rest of the chapter puts flesh and bone on it. We discover that faith is not the absence of doubt. For example, Abraham and Sarah did remarkable things by faith (Hebrews 11:8-12). Abraham also nudged his wife into the arms of another man because he didn't trust God to do right by him—twice (Genesis 12; 20)! Then we have Sarah, the woman with the chutzpah to laugh at God for outlandish promises (Genesis 18:9-15). And let's spare ourselves the comedy routine of Jacob's faith.

If Hebrews 11 teaches us anything, it is that faith has little to do with certainty and more to do with a willingness to act faithfully despite uncertainty—an idea we shall return to later.

MICROSCOPES AND TELESCOPES

The technical term for what I was experiencing as I sorted through all of this is an "epistemological crisis." Crises of faith come in all shapes and sizes, but an epistemological crisis occurs when you realize that *what* you think about the world (your conclusions) isn't half as big an issue as *how* you think about the world (your methods). You realize you don't just have the wrong answer, but you are using the wrong equation. You realize you didn't just misidentify a specimen on the petri dish, but you need to trade in your microscope for a telescope.

We are hardwired to choose the path of least resistance and seek the least dramatic explanation, so when we get things wrong, we might acknowledge it but remain confident that the way we make sense of the world is basically sound. Our conclusions can be wrong, but our methods are sure. Our microscope is all we need. Oh, we might misinterpret the Bible from time to time, but we can (and should) be certain that appealing to the Bible and nothing but the Bible is the sure and proper way to find the whole truth and nothing but the truth. *Sola scriptura!* (Scripture alone!)—as our Reformation fathers would say. (To be sure, the best and brightest Reformers knew *sola scriptura* was a hyperbolic way to say *prima scriptura*—the primacy of Scripture over tradition—but much folk Protestant theology has taken the hyperbolic slogan hyperliterally and believes the Bible, by itself, can deliver a sure and certain faith.)

And I, for one, really wish things were that simple. I wish all the pieces of a perfect faith effortlessly fell into place as I read the Bible with an open mind and generous heart. But things are not that simple, primarily because the Bible is not and was never meant to be anyone's ticket to certainty, nor is it "self-authenticating" in the way many would like to think. History has born this out. For example, we Protestants tend to fancy ourselves a particularly biblical kind of Christian, and yet from the very beginning we have not been able to agree how to interpret what the Bible says, even on matters as fundamental as the Eucharist! It's no small wonder that at last count there are somewhere around forty thousand Protestant Christian denominations. The results are in—the Bible alone has proven every bit as incapable as reason alone in producing the truth, the whole truth, sure and certain.

When the epistemological rug is pulled out from under us and we are confronted with our basic fallibility (or humanity) and the inadequacy of Scripture alone or reason alone or anything alone, we have a decision to make. Some double down on their own certainty and spit into the wind of uncertainty in an attempt to restore the "innocence" that has been lost. We don't need telescopes! *Sola microscopio!* This is the basic pathology of fundamentalism.

Years ago, I had lunch with someone trying to double down on his own certainty, though I did not perceive it at the time. He was a smart and kind young man who asked a string of questions about Genesis and the age of the earth and the logistics of fitting all those animals on the ark. I asked him where the questions were coming from and why he found them so concerning, and while he claimed he was searching for ways to convince hostile coworkers, I think, with hindsight, he was trying to convince himself. So I offered him a telescope—some thoughts on how a proper reading of any literature must respect its genre, and how the genre of Genesis's primeval history is not history in the modern sense. But none of this satisfied him, because he was looking for something else: his lost certainty and innocence. He was looking for a return to a simpler world where he didn't know he was an ant. I recognized it because I too had lived it. Innocence lost recognizes innocence lost.

What followed is a scenario many of us have seen and some of us have experienced. He rejected the telescope and gripped his microscope so tightly it broke. His desire for a long-lost certainty led him into a season of obsessive apologetics and hyperfundamentalism. Apologetics has its place (indeed this book is an apologetic of sorts), but when it gets manic it is often the death throes of a doomed faith. People accidentally strangle their own faith because they cannot bring themselves to let it go and see if it can really stand on its own—accidental faith suicide. I was not surprised to learn he walked away from faith (because he felt he had to walk away from his hyperliteralized Bible) shortly thereafter. Studying stars through microscopes is a sure-fire way to become resentful of both stars and microscopes.

The other way to respond when we realize the epistemological emperor isn't wearing any clothes is to accept our basic fallibility and kiss certainty goodbye. This is easy to say yet very hard to do. It requires that both what and how we think about the world will now be more flexible and porous. We do not trash our microscopes, but we learn when to use our telescopes instead. We will pick up other tools along the way, each helping us see reality from a different angle. Learning the art of focusing them all is a dizzying choreography to master. We will be tempted to return to the faux simplicity of *sola microscopio.*

I know it can be excruciating. When I realized the Bible alone could not provide me with invincible, indestructible, certain faith, I feared I was losing my soul. I pined for a return to innocence. I tried to convince myself that I believed all the same things in the exact same way I always had. But once the doubt *really* hits, there is no going back. We cannot unsee what we have seen. We are different now, and our faith, if we are to keep it, will be different too. And that's okay. Don't be afraid. Don't turn on the fluorescent lights. Sit in the dark for a while. Pray. Get back to basics. Accept the journey your doubt wants to take you on. Accept the journey Jesus wants to take you on using your doubts: "Brothers and sisters, stop thinking like children. In regard to evil be infants, but in your thinking be adults" (1 Corinthians 14:20 NIV).

I am trying. I am trying to stop convincing myself. I am trying to stop tipping the scales. I am trying to stop using faith to seek certainty. I am an ant on a rollercoaster, and when I accept that and throw my hands up in equal portions terror, bliss, and surrender, the real magic of faith begins.

CHAPTER THREE

HOW TO SURVIVE A HURRICANE

DOUBTING WITH JOB

*E*verything nailed down is coming loose."

In 2005, a superstorm rumbled through the Gulf of Mexico, and for the first time in fifty years, my small hometown of Lufkin, Texas, experienced an honest-to-God hurricane. Nestled deep in the piney woods, we were hundreds of miles inland, and the storm weakened considerably before it reached us, but Hurricane Rita was still strong enough to keep us on edge, topple a towering pine tree, and crash it into my grandparents' dining room. Everything nailed down (even an ancient pine tree) came loose.

The Bible is filled with stories of everything nailed down coming loose. God is not always the sanctuary (Psalm 46:1). Sometimes God is the storm:

> The voice of the Lord is upon the waters;
> The God of glory thunders,
> The Lord is over many waters.
> The voice of the Lord is powerful,
> The voice of the Lord is majestic.
> The voice of the Lord breaks the cedars;
> Yes, the Lord breaks in pieces the cedars of Lebanon. . . .
> The voice of the Lord shakes the wilderness. . . .

The voice of the LORD . . . strips the forests bare.
   (Psalm 29:3-5, 8-9)

God is a very present help in times of trouble. God is also a hurricane. A biblical character named Job knows this better than most, and he taught me how to survive a hurricane.

JOB

"There was a man in the land of Uz whose name was Job" (Job 1:1).

With this sentence we meet Job and step into his story—perhaps the most fascinating story in the Bible. Job is not an Israelite name, and Uz is not an Israelite territory. These details would grab the attention of early listeners and readers: "Job's archaic name and foreign homeland help to establish a sense of narrative distance." What we are about to read is not a normal tale. It occurs "long, long ago in a place far, far away." Surprises abound.

Job is a book "at odds with itself." It resists elementary explanations and moralizing. It begins with a simple story, veers into a series of sophisticated poetic and theological speeches, then abruptly resolves. In fact, it doesn't resolve as much as it leaves you baffled and suspecting you have missed something, so back to the story you go. For almost a year, I prayed no prayers, I stepped through no church doors, and I did not read a single word from the Bible . . . except for Job.

All is well when we meet Job. He is good, rich, and righteous. But a butterfly flaps its wings up in the heavens, and a hurricane heads his way. God has gathered the heavenly court and takes a moment to dote on Job: "There is no one like him on the earth, a blameless and upright man, fearing God and turning away from evil" (Job 1:8). But there is a skeptic in the assembly—"the accuser" (Hebrew *satan*) suggests Job's righteousness is rooted in crude self-interest:

So do you think Job does all that out of the sheer goodness of his heart? Why, no one ever had it so good! You pamper him like a pet, make sure nothing bad ever happens to him or his family or his possessions, bless everything he does—he can't lose!

But what do you think would happen if you reached down and took away everything that is his? He'd curse you right to your face, that's what. (Job 1:9-11 *The Message*)

God thinks Job is up to the challenge: "Behold, all that he has is in your power, only do not put forth your hand on him" (Job 1:12). The accuser departs to test Job's righteousness, and a string of tragedies, each one more terrible than the last, unfolds.

A band of raiders steals his oxen and donkeys and murders his servants. Then the fire of God falls from heaven and consumes his sheep and his servants. Then another band of raiders steals his camels and murders his servants. Then a whirlwind races across the wilderness and levels the house where his children are gathered. There are no survivors; the loss is total.

Upon receiving this news, Job tears his robe, shaves his head, and falls to the ground in anguished worship. Once he has composed himself enough to speak, he says the most remarkable thing:

Naked I came from my mother's womb,
And naked I shall return there.
The LORD gave and the LORD has taken away.
Blessed be the name of the LORD. (Job 1:21)

As Job watches his life burn to the ground, he praises God. Unfortunately, the accuser is still not convinced of Job's piety, so when the heavenly court reconvenes, he proposes yet another test and God (again!) obliges:

Then Satan went out from the presence of the LORD and smote Job with sore boils from the sole of his foot to the crown of his head. And he took a potsherd to scrape himself while he was sitting among the ashes.

Then his wife said to him, "Do you still hold fast your integrity? Curse God and die!" But he said to her, "You speak as one of the foolish women speaks. Shall we indeed accept good from God and not accept adversity?" In all this Job did not sin with his lips. (Job 2:7-10)

Strangely enough, many people stop reading Job at this point, so they think the moral of the story is something along the lines of "Even if God were to take everything from us, we should praise him just the same and get on with our lives." Praise God, don't doubt, and get over it.

Growing up, I encountered Job numerous times and always walked away with the general sense that it taught heroic and humble worship in the face of absolute loss. Job was promoted as a paragon of faithful suffering. And indeed Job is, but by the end of chapter two we have barely scratched the surface of what faithful suffering entails. "Praise God, don't doubt, and get over it" might be the moral of Job if Job stopped here, but Job's story is just beginning. Those with eyes to see already spy chinks in Job's heroic armor: "His response [in chapters 1 and 2] is sincere, but it will have to reach a deeper level."

For example, Job calls God by a different name after the second calamity. He shifts from the personal name of God in chapter one (*Yahweh* = the LORD) to the formal name of God in chapter two (*Elohim* = God). Have Job's wounds created a relational distance between himself and God? Furthermore, whereas we are told in chapter one that he "did not sin nor did he blame God" (Job 1:22), in chapter two we are told he "did not sin with his lips" (Job 2:10). Why is the qualifier "with his lips" added? Job still says the right thing, but is there now a contrast between what is on his lips and what is in his heart? The Talmud, an ancient collection of Jewish teachings, suggests so, proposing that while Job did not sin with his lips, he did sin in his heart. We do not have to wonder for long.

Three friends hear of his devastation, come to visit, and for seven days they sit silently in Job's ashes. It's difficult for us to imagine seven days of silence, seven days of stewing and simmering without any verbal release. And in those seven days of silence, a hurricane is brewing inside Job—a hurricane every bit as intense as the one that swept through and took everything from him. Things are about to come loose.

JOB TELLS THE TRUTH

"Afterward Job opened his mouth and cursed the day of his birth" (Job 3:1).

These are the words that open chapter three, and we discover that a happy ending is not soon to follow—far from it. What actually follows is a series of speeches, thirty-five chapters long, in which Job and his friends duke it out over suffering, sovereignty, retribution, and how to speak of and to God in the midst of it all. And Job is in a fighting mood:

Therefore I will not keep silent;
    I will speak out in the anguish of my spirit,
    I will complain in the bitterness of my soul. (Job 7:11 NIV)

Know then that God has wronged me
And has closed His net around me. (Job 19:6)

I cry out to you, God, but you do not answer;
    I stand up, but you merely look at me.
You turn on me ruthlessly;
    with the might of your hand you attack me.
You snatch me up and drive me before the wind;
    you toss me about in the storm.
I know you will bring me down to death,
    to the place appointed for all the living. (Job 30:20-23 NIV)

Scandalized by his recklessness and fearing he is losing his faith, Job's well-meaning friends sharply rebuke him. Humans cannot speak to God like this. For them this is a tragic but simple matter: God is just, which means the righteous prosper and the wicked suffer, so Job's outrageous suffering must be the result of Job's wickedness. Job must take it all back, repent, and move on—this is what saints do. Their theological straitjacket permits no other solutions.

There was a time when Job was quite comfortably bridled by this naive manacle, but that time is gone and Job can never don it again. He knows it is a lie. While Job still believes God is just, Job also knows that he is innocent. He did not deserve this. But now Job has backed himself into a corner because as he sits in the ashes and proclaims his innocence, he also implicates God in a damning divine injustice. If Job's outrageous suffering is not a result of his wickedness, then it must be a result of God's wickedness. Either Job is bad or God is bad.

What will he do? Where will he go? His friends beckon him back to the straitjacket. His baser instincts beckon him to apostasy. But Job does neither. Job will cling to God, but he will not do so confined by the suffocating squeeze of simplistic theological straitjackets. He does not know how to escape the corner he has backed himself into, but he will search for a way.

Job and his friends exchange volleys, and it becomes clear that the arguments of Job's friends are stagnant. They are monotonous and sterile. They repeat them over and over, creating nothing but tired ruts. As Gustavo Gutierrez says:

His friends' arguments are like a wheel spinning in air: they do not go anywhere. Theirs is the wasted energy of intellectuals who get excited but do not actually do anything; they are incapable of taking a step forward, because the impulse that makes them string arguments together is purely verbal. Why do they keep arguing, Job will ask . . . if they have nothing to say? The question applies to every theology that lacks a sense of the mystery of God. The self-sufficient talk of these men is the real blasphemy: their words veil and disfigure the face of a God who loves freely and gratuitously. The friends believe in their theology rather than the God of their theology.

By contrast, Job's speeches are innovative; they have elevation and energy. We see him evolving and going places. He has not figured it out, and he does not yet know how to faithfully speak to and of God in light of his cataclysmic situation, but his faith will keep searching. He believes God is just, but he also knows he is innocent, and while he cannot reconcile how both could be true, he will not cower to his friends' sanitized theologizing and phony certitude. Cornered between a straitjacket and a hurricane, Job takes his flickering candle of faith and steps into the tempest. But Job is not *losing* his faith; Job is *expressing* his faith. He is wandering, but he is not lost. He is a rebel, but he is a faithful rebel.

There are many ways to be a saint, and at times our fidelity may look like betrayal. We may have to become "saints of darkness." We may have to be saints whose light seems to go out as we wander in the shadows, saints who tell the truth even when the truth seems blasphemous. Satan is the father of lies, so lying about our doubt and pain, even in the name of piety and reverence, is satanic. Conversely, the truth, even when impious and irreverent, can free us. Saint Job is proof, and at the end of his story he gets what he asked for: a showdown with the divine.

The showdown both does and does not go as we would expect. God comes in a hurricane and asks Job a few questions of his own, questions intended to remind Job he's an ant on a rollercoaster. God says many things, but the one thing God never does is give Job a straight answer to his questions. Some of the things ripped loose are never nailed back down. The way of God is wild and mysterious, and we must learn to live with unanswered questions and open wounds, and this much we expect and must accept. But then comes something we do not expect.

"Job spoke rightly of me."

After putting Job in his ant-sized place, this is what God says (Job 42:7, 8). Job—who assailed God with accusations of injustice, indifference, and malice—spoke rightly. But Job's friends—who told him to praise God, don't doubt, and get over it—spoke wrongly, *and* God's wrath is kindled against them. What could this mean? How has Job spoken rightly? He has said terrible things. He has been divinely reprimanded.

Understandably, many get confused here and fall back on a very flat reading of Job's story: Job has spoken rightly in the sense that he finally repents of his blasphemies and submits to the sovereignty of God (Job 42:1-6). He is a hero in Job 1–2, villain in Job 3–41, and then hero again in Job 42. He praises God, repents of doubt, and gets over it.

But if this were the case, such commendable behavior would be what Job's friends have been advocating the entire time:

> Can you discover the depths of God? Can you discover the limits of the Almighty? . . . What can you do? . . . If you would direct your heart right . . . your life would be brighter than noonday. (Job 11:7-8, 13, 17)

So how have the friends spoken wrongly and why are they now objects of divine wrath (Job 42:7-9)? A flat, prosaic reading obscures the form and function of Job. The story of Job is not the story of a man who had faith, lost it, then found it again. It is, taken as a whole, the story of a man of tremendous faith, fighting like hell to keep his faith.

I do not know everything that is meant when God declares Job has spoken rightly, but surely it is a testimony to Job's honesty and courage:

> God's approval evidently refers to Job's speeches as a whole, to the entire way he has followed. . . . These speeches do not lack for bold expressions that spring from the depths of Job's suffering and from the torment he feels at not being able to understand what has happened to him. But these bold expressions do not prevent God's agreement and approval; God does not accuse Job either of sin in his earlier life or of blasphemy in what he has said.

Job does not always speak accurately or piously, but he does speak honestly and courageously. He has the courage to tell the truth even when others claim that truth damns him. While his friends are busy talking *about* God, Job talks *to* God. His friends theorize about the hurricane from a distance; Job stands in the eye of the storm. Job encounters the divine; his friends do not.

I have heard of You by the hearing of the ear;

But now my eye sees You. (Job 42:5)

Job's gospel saved my faith because it taught me to stop trying to convince myself I don't have doubts and start telling the truth about them. It taught me that I don't have to fear my doubts. They are not a virtue or a vice, they're not something to be proud of ashamed of, and they don't make me a saint or a sinner. Job taught me to take my doubts and tell the truth because that is the first step toward being faithful with them. Telling the truth about them means you take God too seriously to let doubt fester and rot you from the inside. I can't say it better than Miguel de Unamuno has: "Those who believe that they believe in God, but without any passion in their heart, without anguish of mind, without uncertainty, without doubt, without an element of despair even in their consolation, believe only in the idea of God, not in God Himself."

The times are and are always a-changin', and faith must always evolve. Faith evolves or it dies. Most of the people I've seen walk away from faith are not those who expressed doubt but those who refused to express their doubts until it was too late. This is because your doubts can tell when you're anxiously policing them, when you're not playing fair, when you're full of it; and they will hold your faith hostage until you let them have their say. None of this speaks to the modern enchantment with the cathartic powers of self-expression so much as it speaks to the ancient notion that we are heirs of Israel—the people who wrestle with God (Genesis 32:24-32). In other words, faith's evolution is really just a return to its roots. Christians tell the truth and tell it to God, and the church should be the most honest place in the world. Church should be a place where the real erupts.

KEEP THE CONVERSATION GOING

The first funeral I officiated was for an eighteen-year-old girl killed in a car accident. To this day I've never experienced a more difficult funeral. And as I spoke and looked out into a sea of grief, one face stood out—that of her boyfriend. I met with him shortly after the funeral and learned that days before the accident he had purchased an engagement ring and had been planning to propose.

Neither of us spoke much during that initial meeting; words felt treasonous. But in the meetings that followed, we gradually opened up to one another, and he asked me how to deal with all the anger and grief. He told me prayer had never come easily for him. He never knew how to talk to God, and at this particular moment he had nothing nice to say. So I gave him a Bible, put a small bookmark in Job 1, and suggested this was a good place to start. We met a few weeks later, and when I asked him how the reading was going he said, "I didn't know we could talk to God like that. If I can talk to God like that, maybe I can talk to God."

Hurricanes come, and if praise is the only language you can speak, you will often find yourself speechless and imploding. We must learn the language of lament so we can give voice to our faith when praise just won't do. We must speak to God even when we don't have anything nice to say. We must keep the conversation going.

If you spend much time around my household or come to me for guidance, then you will hear this over and over: keep the conversation going. You're angry? You're confused? You don't have any faith? Tell God about it. You feel like a fool telling God about it when you doubt he exists, much less cares? Tell God about it: "If the truth is worth telling, it is worth making a fool of yourself to tell." When Jesus felt godforsaken, hanging broken on a cross, he told the truth about it (Matthew 27:46).

I haven't made many explicit vows to God in my life, but one vow I have made and am hell-bent on fulfilling is this: never to *think* something about God that I don't also *say* to God. If I think it, I will pray it. I will tell God about how I feel about God. I will give my doubts no quarter. I will always keep the conversation going. If I crash and burn, I will go down telling God the truth.

How do you survive a hurricane? Don't run from it. Stand your ground. Lean into it. If you survive, let it be because God is God and not because you played it safe.

CHAPTER FOUR

BEAUTIFUL, TERRIBLE WORLD

THE BURDEN OF REALITY

*A*eschylus was the founding father of Greek tragedy. He believed life was vicious, the gods were brutal, and all were doomed to meet a tragic end, either at the hand of fate or the gods, neither of which cared about the sickness unto death that is the pitiable plight of human life.

As legend has it, Aeschylus was walking around one day when an eagle soared overhead, a turtle in its talons, hoping to crack its shell and enjoy a tasty meal. As misfortune would have it, Aeschylus's bald, shiny dome caught the eagle's eye, and mistaking it for a rock, the eagle dropped the turtle from high in the heavens, and poor Aeschylus met (or didn't meet) his maker by way of a turtle dropped from the heavens.

Perhaps life is an amusing but brutal tragedy—humans in the hands of angry gods or fate's cold indifference. As Bono sings, a look into the heavens can produce awe or send a shiver down your spine:

The stars are bright, but do they know?
The universe is beautiful but cold.

In December 2004, something happened deep in the belly of the earth. For a brief moment, two plates broke free and ripped past each other, causing an earthquake that vibrated the whole earth a centimeter and sent tsunamis rushing in all directions with waves a hundred feet high. Few had any warning, and 230,000 people were instantly swallowed up that day by the sea. Things like this can make a good God difficult to believe in.

In his masterpiece *The Brothers Karamazov*, Fyodor Dostoyevsky offers a nuclear critique of Christianity by simply contemplating the suffering of children—a critique far more damning than anything modern scientific atheism could ever proffer. Ivan Karamazov, one of the novel's chief figures, sits in a pub across from his pure-hearted, aspiring-priest younger brother, and reels off a litany of stories about the torture and murder of children—true stories that Dostoyevsky had gathered over the years.

Infants ripped from their mother's arms by soldiers, tossed into the air, and then impaled on bayonets. Babies coaxed into a smile by the silvery shimmer of a gun barrel, and then shot in the face in front of their parents. A little boy hunted down and torn to pieces by dogs. A little girl tortured by her own parents—locked in a freezing outhouse, mouth filled with excrement because she wet the bed. Ivan dares his priestly brother (and us) to envision that little girl and asks, "Can you understand why a little creature, who can't even understand what's done to her, should beat her little aching heart with her tiny fist in the dark and the cold, and weep her meek unresentful tears to dear, kind God to protect her? Do you understand . . . you pious and humble novice?"

And where is dear, kind God when all of this is happening? How many children died of starvation since I started writing this chapter? How many wives of cancer? How many geriatrics of loneliness, lost in the haze of time and misfiring neurons, long ago forgotten by friends and family? A turtle falls from the heavens, the doors of the sea burst open, a child whimpers alone in the dark, and the world carries on without mercy or pity or the slightest pangs of conscience. Meanwhile, God does nothing.

God's apparent apathy would not be a problem were it not for the fact that Christianity proclaims a God of infinite power and beauty, a God presumably able and willing to do something instead of nothing.

At a conference, a man stood and asked Alvin Plantinga, veteran of decades in the philosophical academy, if he could think of any good reason not to believe in God. Plantinga thought for a moment and then curtly responded, "No—not really." The friendly crowd chuckled, and Plantinga smiled but then wryly added, "Well—perhaps the problem of evil."

The problem of evil.

BEAUTY AND BRUTALITY

I remember when evil was just a "problem" for me. For the first twenty-nine years of my life, evil was just a "problem." Don't get me wrong. I experienced my share of suffering, and loved ones died, and I struggled to make sense of it—standard human stuff. But even though it was, quite literally, a matter of life and death, it wasn't a matter of life and death for my faith. I struggle explaining it, but perhaps you know what I mean.

I knew evil was a problem. I could spell out the syllogism:

- God is all-powerful.
- God is all-good.
- An all-powerful and good God would not allow evil.
- Evil is.

Or as Epicurus allegedly put it, perhaps prompted by Aeschylus's fatal collision with a free-falling reptilian harbinger of Hades: Is God willing to prevent evil, but not able? Then he is impotent. Is he able, but not willing? Then he is malevolent. Is he both able and willing? Whence then is evil?

And yet the "problem" of evil never managed to get under my skin and down into by bones. I am a measured, logical person, and so long as I had measured, logical answers, evil was and would ever remain just a "problem" and as such, no real problem for my faith. But one day something happened—something wonderful and re-markable and jubilant beyond measure (it remains the happiest moment of my life) and something that nearly shipwrecked my faith.

My son was born.

On September 30, 2014, we welcomed Wyatt Thomas Fischer into the world. He was five days early, but we didn't mind. I'll never forget the first time I touched him. He came out screaming, our doctor handled him gently and placed him in the bedside bassinet to clean him up. His little hands were thrust up into the air, palms open, reaching out. Instinctively, I put my two index fingers into his tiny, reaching hands (one in each palm), and he latched on. The world was now a different place.

And everything was fine—no complications. Both of our families and many of our friends were there. We took him home, and apart from your garden-variety parental insomnia, everything was fine. And in some sense, there is no *but* coming. He's a happy, healthy, rambunctious little boy—far happier and healthier than we could have ever wished. He is a constant (if sometimes *too* constant) source of joy. Daily, I look back and realize that before him I was like the Grinch, living with a heart "three sizes too small." And daily my heart grows a little bigger. And this is when evil slowly started becoming more than a problem.

There is a direct correlation between our ability to apprehend beauty and our ability to apprehend brutality, between our sensitivity to bliss and our sensitivity to suffering. The more we see the world ablaze with the love of God, the more we see the world on fire, burning to the ground, consumed by sin, suffering, and death. I suppose I should have known that (and perhaps I did "know" it), but I was not prepared for what it would mean. I was not prepared to live with a bigger heart beating inside my chest.

On the one hand, the world had never been brighter: a theater of boundless revelry and grace, a mirror in which we glimpse the beauty of the infinite. Look into a child's eyes, and there's no telling what wonders you might see reflected back. As David Bentley Hart has said,

> Creation's being is God's pleasure, creation's beauty God's glory; beauty reveals the shining of an uncreated light . . . upon all things, a *claritas* that discloses the lineaments of what it infuses and shows them to be the firm outlines of that weight, that *kabod*, that proclaims God's splendor; it is the coincidence of forms upon the surface of being and the infinite depths of divine light of which all form partakes . . . the bounteousness of God's goodness standing "outside" itself.

Or in plainer terms, all that is arises from nothing and without necessity and is sustained, moment by moment, by the superabundant source of being that is God. Existence itself is grace—a gift, unforeseen and unnecessary and gratuitous, given anew in the unfolding of each moment in which there is something instead of nothing. And not only is there something, but there are so many beautiful somethings: sunrises and stars and smiles, meadows and mimosas and mercy, the small, smooth pebble and the craggiest peak.

There is a small Catholic retreat center a few miles from my house, tucked away in a thick grove of cedar and oak trees. Follow the prayer trail on the back of the property, and it eventually leads to a hidden canyon. Not the Grand Canyon, but still canyon enough to make you feel little and loved and thankful. When Wyatt was a few months old, my wife and I took him there for the first time. It was spring and the canyon was alive. Squirrels scurrying after their long nap, wildflowers preening, birds floating on the warm breeze, and trees being trees—twisted branches stretching in all directions, flush with green leaves. Who knew green could come in so many colors! That little canyon put on its show, and we watched and gratefully wondered why such things should even exist.

Some of Job's happier words came to mind: "Where were you when I laid the foundation of the earth? . . . When the morning stars sang together and all the sons of God shouted for joy?" (Job 38:4, 7). In those moments, we were joining together with the morning stars and sons of God in a sacred, rambunctious hymn of praise.

Yet as the light grew ever brighter, the dark grew ever darker, and on April 25, 2015, I discovered the depth of my inner darkness.

HERE IS THE WORLD

"Another earthquake will probably happen soon."

I didn't think about it much when he said it.

In March 2015, I was in Nepal teaching at a pastor's training conference and visiting a few orphanages, and had just finished a hike to Shivapuri—a summit in the hills surrounding the Kathmandu Valley. Exhausted and a bit nauseous due to the bumpy drive down, I vaguely remember my conversation with our guide.

Kathmandu is densely populated—buildings upon buildings. When you run out of room, you start building up, and that was what worried our guide. Every seventy years or so, a colossal earthquake hits Nepal. The fault line that produces the majesty of the Himalayas also produces big earthquakes. Beauty and brutality. He knew an earthquake was overdue and that when it happened, the damage would be catastrophic.

He was the first person I thought of when I woke up on April 25 and looked at my phone. Because it was Saturday, I was in no rush to get out of bed, but the incessant pinging of my phone irritated me enough to make me search for the source of such a commotion.

An earthquake had hit Nepal—a big earthquake. The official death toll at that moment was 111, but I knew it would rise. A month earlier, I had seen the buildings upon buildings, and now I shuddered as I imagined them tumbling down.

The second person I thought of was a group of people—children at the orphanages we had visited. Many of their stories would have provided more kindling for Ivan Karamazov's fire. One little girl possessed the most radiant smile I have ever seen and was placed in the orphanage because her starving mother tried to kill and eat her. Putting that into words feels perverse, but it is her truth and it is the truth and so our truth must find a place for it.

What if her building collapsed? Face after face invaded my mind as I considered the unthinkable.

Right about then, my wife walked into the bedroom with Wyatt for what had become my favorite ritual—him crawling around on me, grinning from ear to ear and babbling about how extraordinary he found any and every thing. Sunshine cascaded through the windows. My brother-in-law was getting married that afternoon, and I was performing the ceremony.

I sat with my son, a day of bliss in front of us. These moments make faith easy. Of course it's all going to be okay. Of course there is a God of limitless love beyond the walls of the world. No other explanation will suffice. But on the other side of the world, fathers are digging through rubble for their sons. Worse yet, many children lie beneath the rubble who don't have parents to look for them. What can one say in such moments? Maybe we can only say what Frederick Buechner has said: "Here is the world. Beautiful and terrible things will happen."

I had always known terrible things happened, but there and then I experienced, for the first time, something I find difficult to explain—a flash of sublime, transcendent empathy. I was there in the rubble of Kathmandu, looking for all these orphaned children of God. And I was there in the bottomless rubble of history, looking for all the orphaned children of God. And I understood that I understood nothing. Ivan Karamazov's taunt echoed: "Can you understand, you pious and humble novice?" No, I cannot. I do not want to.

One of the blessings and curses of being a pastor is that, regardless of how you feel, you must show up to church Sunday after Sunday. I have never despised worship like I did that next day. I was in the middle of a sermon series called "Skeptics Welcome!" (not kidding) but had scheduled a break because a Nepali pastor friend (also not kidding) was in town and I wanted him to speak to us about his work there. Clearly he was in no state to take the stage, so we had another friend fill in. We raised a good chunk of money for earthquake relief. We sang hopeful songs. I watched and listened and have never before or since felt so dead inside.

THE BURDEN OF REALITY

"Can we carry the burden of reality?"

My life since April 25, 2015, has been an open-ended exploration of that question. Can we really afford to know how deep the world's misery runs? Could we smile anymore if we did? When reality's wretchedness erupts through the wallpaper, can we see it without being blinded?

How much reality can we bear and remain human? I used to think myself somewhat invincible in these regards. Bring on reality, all of it! I can take it. I have since learned I cannot. It is too heavy and there is too much. I now agree with Henri Nouwen: "Maybe we have to be tolerant towards our own avoidances and denials in the conviction that we cannot force ourselves to face what we are not ready to respond to and in the hope that in one future day we will have the courage and strength to open our eyes fully and see without being destroyed." And I think Stanley Cavell says more than he knows when he observes, "Only a God, or the son of God, could bear being human."

I kept quiet about my darkness. I shared bits and pieces with my wife and a few close friends, but always felt silly doing so. I criticized myself internally even as I spoke: "So you just realized the world can be nasty? You haven't seen anything. Imagine if you had been digging through the rubble for your son. Get a grip."

I tried to get a grip, to convince myself I was being unreasonable and overly sentimental. "The world is fallen; people die. Don't let the tears obscure the facts. You know there are answers to the problem of evil."

I tried to pray and preach myself out of the dark, but the harder I tried, the bleaker the situation became. And then finally, I stopped trying—not because God told me to but because I was so exhausted I had no choice. I stopped trying to force the light and pretend the dark wasn't really that dark. I let myself envision the blasphemous and felt the chill of a world without God. Eventually, a word came to me—not all at once, but little by little: *surrender*.

I sensed God saying, "Surrender to the dark. Feel its weight and its chill. Accept that evil will never again be just a problem for you. Accept that you will never understand it, that it would be far worse if you did." To extend the Buechner quote from earlier, "Here is the world. Beautiful and terrible things will happen. Don't be afraid."

THE TRIAL OF GOD

I can offer no perfect prescriptions. I can only describe the road I traveled and am still traveling, and on this road I am learning we haven't the slightest clue what kind of problem evil is until we understand it is much more than a problem. It is a crisis. The world should stop turning each time we bury a child. And if it does not, that means our hearts are three sizes too small and we have swapped the gospel for something that causes us less pain because it offers us less hope. When Jesus stood before the tomb of his friend and wept, he was not being sentimental (John 11:35). He was being human. He was also being divine.

The paradoxical crisis of evil is that it makes us wonder both if we can live with God and if we can live without God. One is reminded of the "trial of God." On a cold winter evening in Auschwitz, three rabbis put God on trial for crimes against creation and his people. God was found guilty and after an "infinity of silence," one of the prosecuting rabbis looked into the sky: "It's time for evening prayers." So the rabbis huddled together and prayed to the God they had just indicted. I think God understood; perhaps he was pleased.

Christianity sows seeds of celestial charity in our hearts, and those seeds can mutate into an existential brokenheartedness on behalf of the suffering world. The radiance of divine love can morph into a tumor that destroys faith. Christian faith creates a love so fierce that it can accidently subvert faith in the name of love in the face of savage evil. In other words, it is often those with deep faith, firmly grounded in the love of God, who find their faith languishing in the shadows when faced with creation's ceaseless pain: "The more a person believes, the more deeply he experiences pain over the suffering of the world."

Sometimes it is our faith that makes us feel we are losing our faith. A crisis of faith in the face of evil can be the truest expression of faith, because what we interpret as a loss of faith is often the growing pains of learning to live with a heart three sizes larger beating inside our chest. So if evil (almost) makes us lose our faith, it might be because our faith is growing strong, not growing weak.

And yet while evil makes being a Christian near unbearable at times, it also makes being something else near unthinkable. All things considered, the only thing worse than the "problem" of evil is not having the "problem" of evil. Imagine evil not being God-damnable. Imagine standing over a child's grave and not being able to call it *evil* because your worldview lacks a category for evil. Imagine not being able to call senseless torture *evil* because you think the heavens are empty and our deepest moral intuitions of justice and goodness are utilitarian fictions of the human mind, accidental residues of evolutionary processes.

Convince yourself there is no God. Convince yourself we have evolved beyond good and evil. Convince yourself our desire for everlasting life and justice is only a survival tactic, a way to better carry on the mindless task of spreading our seed and passing on genes. Abolish God and embrace the world for the cold, brute event it is.

It will not help. Your child will die or you will experience gratuitous suffering, and it will be a crisis. You will be furious and broken, and curse the empty heavens, and evil will remain every bit the problem it was before. Abolish God and your burning hatred of evil will still smolder unabated, which ought to tell you something. Besides, sanguine repose before creation's pain is more cowardly than it is heroic.

Our choice is believing everything or denying everything: "My brothers, a time of testing has come for us all. We must believe everything or deny everything. And who among you, I ask, would dare to deny everything?"

As a Christian, I believe that the truth (grounded in the Trinity and revealed in Jesus Christ) is not only true but also good and beautiful. I think that beauty is "a measure of what theology may call true." The truth is beautiful and beauty is the truth. And so I've come to believe that a faith's truthfulness might be best determined by the degree to which evil is a problem for it. Given the steely fact of evil, I am grateful my faith causes a crisis instead of a shoulder shrug. And amid all the world's brutality, this is the beauty of Christian faith: it has made a good many of us incapable of seeing evil as anything other than evil and assured that our eyes will never be dry standing over the grave of a child. We have been taught to hope for too much to settle for less. We survey the rubble, ponder deserting Jesus, but when he asks whether or not we're leaving we say, "Lord, where else could we go?" (John 6:68). We are destined to die with broken hearts and would have it no other way.

I do not understand evil and hope I never do. I bear my share of reality. I tell God the truth. The optics have changed, and I see a wider and deeper range of colors than I did before—brighter brights and darker darks. Evil will never again be a problem but always a crisis and for that I say, "Thanks be to God." Most of the time, I mean it.

GOD OF THE GALLOWS

Nobel Peace Prize winner Elie Wiesel lived through the Holocaust. His memoir, *Night*, is filled with heartbreaking stories we wish we could forget, but one is especially unforgettable.

A young boy is sentenced to death, accused of participating in a conspiracy. The guards commenced the usual execution ritual— preparing the gallows and gathering the prisoners. Executions were normal, but the execution of a child was not. The guards were noticeably nervous. Wiesel watches in a state of numbed horror as the noose is placed around the boy's neck. Behind him, he hears someone muttering, "Where is merciful God? Where is He?"

The chair is kicked over and the little boy hangs. The prisoners weep. The guards vainly feign stoicism. As is custom, the prisoners are then marched past the victim, who is typically dead at that point. But the little boy is too light to asphyxiate quickly, so he hangs for more than half an hour, "lingering between life and death, writhing before our eyes." As Wiesel walks by the boy, he recalls what happened:

> Behind me, I heard the same man asking:
> "For God's sake, where is God?"
> And from within me, I heard a voice answer:
> "Where He is? This is where—hanging here from this gallows."

There is God—hanging from the gallows.

Wiesel's meaning is clear: his faith in God hangs on those gallows with the little boy. He has seen too much, shouldered too much reality, and has been undone. Who could blame him?

I cannot blame him, but while I honor Wiesel's meaning, I have always been drawn to another meaning, perhaps further up and further in. There is God—hanging from the gallows. It is not a moment of divine absence but divine presence. God is *there*, hanging—not a very divine thing to do. This is the great mystery of incarnation and crucifixion: God takes on flesh and suffers with us. It is not an answer to the question of suffering. It is a reminder that God has born the full weight of sorrow, for only a God or the son of God could bear being human. It is a reminder that "instead of explaining our suffering God shares it."

Even in his resurrected body, we are told Jesus keeps the holes of the crucifixion nails in his hands and the spear in his side, and it is by these wounds that Thomas recognizes him (John 20:26-28). So I've often wondered, if Jesus kept the holes where the nails entered his hands and the spear entered his side, surely he kept the hole where the spear entered his heart. Surely Jesus, even now, is God with a hole in his heart. And perhaps it is by this wound, preserved eternally in the heart of God, that we recognize him.

Why, God, would you permit such? Why permit such suffering for yourself, for us? I do not know, I might never know, and yet, there is God—hanging from the gallows. God with a hole in his heart.

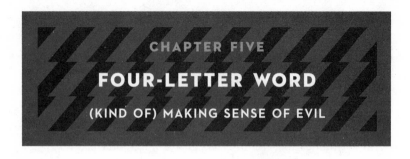

*W*e should not understand evil. It is not a problem to be solved. It is a crisis to be endured.

Any Christian reflections on evil must start here because, as John Polkinghorne has claimed, "Ultimately, responding to the surd of tragedy requires the insights of the poet more than the arguments of the logician." Anyone who can coolly, calmly discuss evil isn't really reckoning with it. But a world with all poets and no logicians would be insufferably sentimental, so while we should never truly *understand* evil, we will inevitably aspire to make some sense of it. Humans are hardwired to ask *why*, especially when faced with evil: "It is not really a question at all, in the sense of something we can ask or not ask. . . . It is *the open wound of life* in this world." When the tears dry and we find our voices again, we must speak, even if only in chastened whispers. Because while speaking may be sinning, may be mocking the dead, it appears to be a sin we need to commit at some point.

As a pastor, I have learned not to speak while the ashes still smolder. I show up, I hug, I weep. This is not always easy—oftentimes the wounded themselves offer the pious platitudes, desperately seeking to find comfort in connecting providential dots. Who could blame them? I don't correct them, but I don't indulge it either. I listen and nod and remind them Jesus loves them and weeps with them.

But there is a time to speak about evil, and what can we say then? How can we make sense of the crisis without blaspheming by claiming to understand or solve the "problem"? Two stories—tried through the furnace of history, attested to in Scripture, passed down by the church— give us the grammar and plot to venture forward in faith, hope, and love.

TWO SONS AND TWO FATHERS

In 1968, a young man named David Koop was climbing a mountain when he slipped and fell to his death. A few years later, his father, Everett Koop, wrote a book reflecting on his son's tragic death, and he offers this remarkable assessment: "We believe that from the beginning of time God's plan called for David to climb . . . and to die in that particular, awful way. . . . David's feet did not slip! God took him. . . . That was how David died. God shook the hill, and a piece of the cliff carried him to his death. His feet did not slip."

Fifteen years later, a young man named Eric Wolterstorff was climbing a mountain when he slipped and fell to his death. A few years later, his father, Nicholas Wolterstorff, released a book reflecting on his son's tragic death, and he mentions reading Koop's book and how it incensed him:

> The only thing that angered me in what people offered was a small book someone gave me written by a father whose son had also been killed in a mountaineering accident. The writer [Koop] said that . . . his son's foot had not slipped. *God* had shaken the mountain. God had decided that it was time for him to come home.
> I find this pious attitude deaf to the message of the Christian gospel. . . . The Bible speaks instead of God's *overcoming* death. . . . God is appalled by death.

Two grieving fathers try to make sense of two dead sons, and while their stories are so similar, the stories they tell to make sense of their stories are so different. In one story, God moves the mountain; in the other story, God does not. Layer upon layer of explanation both precede and follow this naked piece of the plot, but there is no mistaking this fundamental point of divergence.

And these two specific stories embody the two big stories Scripture tells as the people of God—channeled through the writers of Scripture and inspired by their maker—try to make sense of the crisis of evil. While they may imply principles and invite some systematizing, we must remember that they are stories (or better yet, metastories), or else we inevitably reduce evil to a problem and reduce Scripture to a book of "waiting to be systematized unsystematic theology." Scripture is not a jumbled puzzle with every piece accounted for, waiting to be put into place. Scripture is not an equation that, worked properly, factors out without remainders. Scripture is a collection of stories that tells us the truth, gives us a plot to live by, and brings us into relationship with the living God. In the case of evil, the many stories of Scripture can form two different mosaics of meaning—two big stories to make sense of the little stories.

STORY #1: EVIL, SOVEREIGNTY, AND THE GLORY OF GOD

In Genesis 45, we witness a family reunion. Joseph, the forgotten son, stands before the brothers who sold him into slavery, weeping so loudly it echoes down the halls of the palace. Drawing them close, he explains why, despite their betrayal, they should not feel guilty:

> Now do not be grieved or angry with yourselves, because you sold me here, for God sent me before you to preserve life. For the famine *has been* in the land these two years, and there are still five years in which there will be neither plowing nor harvesting. God sent me before you to preserve for you a remnant

in the earth, and to keep you alive by a great deliverance. Now, therefore, it was not you who sent me here, but God; and He has made me a father to Pharaoh and lord of all his household and ruler over all the land of Egypt. (Genesis 45:5-8)

Joseph's brothers sold him into slavery, but in some other, truer sense, God had done it. "It was not you—it was God," says Joseph. Paul Helm notes that, according to Joseph, God brought certain evil events to pass "without himself being implicated in the evil, and without diminishing in any way the evil of what was done to Joseph and the responsibility for that evil." And, so says the great nineteenth-century theologian Charles Hodge, "What is true of the history of Joseph is true of all history." In other words, this small story of evil in Joseph's life is also the big story of evil in creation at large—a big story of evil, sovereignty, and the glory of God.

The core plot contends that while God neither does nor is responsible for evil, God does ordain any and all evil that exists. Mark Talbot explains it in this way:

Scripture repudiates the claim that God *does* evil while at the same time everywhere implying that God *ordains* any evil there is. To say that God "ordains" something is to say that he has planned and purposed and willed it from before the creation of the world. . . . Nothing—no evil thing or person or event or deed—falls outside God's ordaining will. . . . So when even the worst of evils befall us, they do not ultimately come from anywhere other than God's hand.

What does it mean for God to ordain evil and yet not do it? Raconteurs of this story—people like Augustine, Calvin, Edwards, and Piper—vary in their explanations, but the bottom line is the same: God ordains it but is not responsible for it.

Why? Why would God ordain evil? Though surely deeply conflicted about it, why would God, in some sense, want evil? Once again, explanations vary but converge around the idea of God's glory.

Notes from the Tilt-a-Whirl is a delightfully rambunctious book, and in it N. D. Wilson provides one of the more evocative narrations of why evil exists and how it does so for the glory of God. He likens it to a famous picture taken by Ansel Adams called "Jeffrey Pine, Sentinel Dome." It is a simple picture, consisting of a tree, the sky, and a rock, and Wilson feels it tells the story of the universe.

The tree is gnarled and bent over double in the face of the invisible but relentless wind. The dome of the heavens stretches out above, and the tree's roots claw down into the granite. The wind will win, but not today; the beauty is in the fight. The picture is in black and white.

Black and white.

Beauty requires contrast, struggle, tension, antithesis, counterpoint. Get rid of all darkness and what do you have? A blank page. Thus Wilson writes, "Could we improve this picture? . . . Remove the tension and the contrast. Remove the black. All of it. Remove the struggle and the inevitable end. Leave the white. Only white. And now it is perfect. Perfectly blank."

Evil is the foil to God's goodness, and without it we cannot perceive the surfeit luminosity of God's glory. Without a fall, we get no crucifixion. Without hell, we couldn't appreciate heaven. Without sin, we never see God's wrath and mercy. Eden is nice, but without a snake or two it would be boring. Kittens are cute, and I suspect they will be in heaven, but so will lions (Isaiah 11:6-7). God ordains evil because he desires the contrast that expresses the full range of his glory, and this is good for us because we were made to experience God's glory from all its tender, rugged, and graphic angles. Wilson continues:

> The shadows exist in the painting, the dark corners of grief and trial and wickedness all exist so that He might step inside them, so we could see how low He can stoop.... Evil exists so that He might be demeaned and insulted, so that the depth of His love and sacrifice could be expressed as much as is possible in the small frame of history.

Along similar lines, the ever-lucid Paul Helm suggests that just "as it is impossible for a person to be forgiven who has not committed a fault, so it is impossible for God to forgive, to show mercy, in a universe in which there is no fault." Or perhaps Edwards says it best: "So evil is necessary, in order to the highest happiness of the creature, and the completeness of that communication of God, for which he made the world." God ordains evil for his glory and our good.

This is one way to tell the story. It has been told for a long time in the church. It has a pile of Scriptures to support it. It has many theological benefactors. It is a biblical, orthodox, Christian attempt to make sense of evil. It is the story I *used* to tell, but now I tell a different story.

STORY #2: EVIL, FREEDOM, AND THE LOVE OF GOD

Genesis 1 claims humans are created in the image of God. This declaration means many things, but its primary point of reference within the actual narrative is humanity's calling to exercise dominion over creation: "Then God said, 'Let Us make man in Our image . . . and let them rule" (Genesis 1:26).

Just as God faithfully rules over the whole of space and time, so humans are to join with him to rule faithfully over a small sliver of reality: the earth. The psalmist joins with Genesis 1:

The heavens are the heavens of the LORD,
But the earth He has given to the sons of men. (Psalm 115:16)

God sovereignly shares his sovereignty. We call this *kenosis*—God pouring himself out in love to make room for another. Father, Son, and Spirit have been doing it eternally. Creation gives us our first glimpse.

Then it all goes to hell. Or to be more precise, some piece of a hell that has already broken loose slithers into the garden.

Genesis 3 narrates the fall of humanity and creation. A clever serpent, later identified as Satan, deceives Adam and Eve into sinning, resulting in a cataclysmic disaster wherein sin is unleashed and thorns and thistles ravage the earth. Or as Saint Paul will say it, creation is enslaved (Romans 8:18-22). All of this leads to an observation so obvious it is usually overlooked—there is no problem of evil in the Bible.

The Bible certainly asks why the righteous suffer and the wicked prosper and why God fails to intervene; however, it never quite addresses the classical problem of evil, defined in terms of the vexing presence of evil in the world of an omnipotent and benevolent Creator. Speaking specifically about the New Testament, Walter Wink says, "The early Christians devoted a great deal of energy to discovering the meaning of Jesus' death, but nowhere do they offer a justification of God in the face of an evil world. They do not seem to be puzzled or even perturbed by evil as a theoretical problem."

How could this be? Were the writers of Scripture too theologically maladroit to perceive the problem? Or do we obsess over it because we've grown too sentimental? As it turns out, neither.

There is no problem of evil in the Bible because the Bible both teaches and assumes, from beginning to end, that the "fall" of Genesis 3 is but symptomatic of a deeper fall, preceding the events in Eden. Where, after all, has that clever serpent come from? Why is Adam told to "guard" the garden (Genesis 2:15 GNT)? Creation languishes in the wake of a primal catastrophe, reaching back before time as we know it, perhaps in a different type of time altogether. And in the aftermath, evil is to be expected because creation is caught in a cosmic war between chaos and peace, evil and good, the "powers and principalities" of this age and the kingdom of heaven, Satan and God (Ephesians 6:12 KJV).

In other words, the writers of Scripture operate with a provisional cosmic dualism of sorts in which there is a real (albeit not eternal) conflict between "a sphere of created autonomy that strives against God on the one hand and the saving love of God in time on the other." Here's a quick flyover tracing this thread.

In Psalms and Isaiah, poets and prophets tell us stories of God taming the forces of chaos in creation. For example, Psalm 74 and Isaiah 51 both speak of God's victory over mythical sea monsters like Leviathan and Rahab:

> You crushed the heads of Leviathan. (Psalm 74:14)
> Was it not You who cut Rahab in pieces,
> Who pierced the dragon? (Isaiah 51:9)

We then have strange Old Testament stories of battles between angels and rival gods. Daniel 10 recounts a vision Daniel receives wherein he learns that kingdoms are watched and warred over by guardian angel "princes":

> Then he said, "Do you understand why I came to you? But I shall now return to fight against the prince of Persia; so I am

going forth, and behold, the prince of Greece is about to come."
(Daniel 10:20)

From here we move to the blatant spiritual warfare of the New
Testament, worth citing more extensively as a reminder of just how
unrelenting it really is:

> And he [the devil] led Him up and showed Him all the
> kingdoms of the world in a moment of time. And the devil
> said to Him, "I will give You all this domain and its glory; for
> it has been handed over to me, and I give it to whomever I
> wish." (Luke 4:5-6)
>
> Now judgment is upon this world; now the ruler of this
> world will be cast out. (John 12:31)
>
> I will not speak much more with you, for the ruler of the
> world is coming, and he has nothing in Me. (John 14:30)
>
> And even if our gospel is veiled, it is veiled to those who are
> perishing, in whose case the god of this world has blinded the
> minds of the unbelieving so that they might not see the light
> of the gospel of the glory of Christ, who is the image of God.
> (2 Corinthians 4:3-4)
>
> And you were dead in your trespasses and sins, in which
> you formerly walked according to the course of this world, ac-
> cording to the prince of the power of the air, of the spirit that
> is now working in the sons of disobedience. (Ephesians 2:1-2)
>
> Finally, be strong in the Lord and in the strength of His might.
> Put on the full armor of God, so that you will be able to stand
> firm against the schemes of the devil. For our struggle is not
> against flesh and blood, but against the rulers, against the powers,
> against the world forces of this darkness, against the spiritual
> *forces* of wickedness in the heavenly *places.* (Ephesians 6:10-12)

We know that we are of God, and that the whole world lies
in *the power of* the evil one. (1 John 5:19)

Move back in time, before the veil of history as we know it is drawn,
and we find cryptic hints of an angelic fall in both Jude and 2 Peter:

And angels who did not keep their own domain, but abandoned
their proper abode, He has kept in eternal bonds under darkness
for the judgment of the great day. (Jude 6)

For if God did not spare angels when they sinned, but cast
them into hell and committed them to pits of darkness, reserved
for judgment. (2 Peter 2:4)

Move forward in time, to the end of time, and the end of the
world as we know it is described in terms of God's victory over Satan:

When the thousand years are completed, Satan will be released
from his prison, and will come out to deceive the nations which
are in the four corners of the earth, Gog and Magog, to gather
them together for the war; the number of them is like the sand
of the seashore. And they came up on the broad plain of the earth
and surrounded the camp of the saints and the beloved city, and
fire came down from heaven and devoured them. And the devil
who deceived them was thrown into the lake of fire and brimstone,
where the beast and the false prophet are also; and they will be
tormented day and night forever and ever. (Revelation 20:7-10)

And all along, the biblical writers never stop to ask why evil exists
because they knew why—the cosmos was at war because created beings
(human and angelic) had abused their God-given freedom and rebelled.
Creation, though good and beautiful, was a battlefield. Cosmic powers
hostile to God rage against God, and humans are both participants
and casualties in the struggle. But why did the cosmic powers fall?

This is a tantalizing question, but the Bible resists speculating on it, perhaps (once again) because the obvious answer need not be spelled out. In a word, *freedom*. God created creatures with a dependent and yet very real autonomy because the "encounter of the finite with the Infinite has to come about by stages," and that autonomy was and is abused. The possibility of such a thing was "the necessary cost of a world allowed to make itself." Any attempts to tease more of an answer out of the Bible will fail because in the Bible, freedom is an ultimate explanation. Creation is an act of love, love requires freedom, freedom requires the *possibility* of evil, and here we hit bedrock—the giving of reasons comes to an end: "Evil and suffering exist because freedom exists; but freedom has no origin; it is an ultimate frontier."

Understandably, we sometimes shrink from this telling of Scripture's big story because we feel it commits us to a form of hokey superstition—spiritual warfare has certainly fallen out of favor in many circles. Or perhaps we shrink from it because we fear it goes too far toward denying divine sovereignty. And while both of these concerns are legitimate and should make us careful and thoughtful, they shouldn't make us miss the deep, biblical precedent of telling the story of Scripture as a story of God's battle against and victory over Satan, sin, and death.

So this is the second primary way to tell the Bible's big story. It has been told for a long time in the church. It has a pile of Scriptures to support it. It has many theological benefactors. It is a biblical, orthodox, Christian attempt to make sense of evil. It's the story I now tell, and here's why.

THUNDER AND LIGHTNING

Some might find it troubling I've conceded that the many small stories of Scripture can be marshaled into two different big stories.

As mentioned earlier, we often feel a deep need for certainty and use the Bible as a means to that end, so no real theological ambiguity can be tolerated. We are uncomfortable with the idea that good, rational people can interpret the Bible differently. We are uncomfortable with the idea that the Bible might not contain *a theology* so much as a number of *theologies*.

Similarly, we often insist on a single biblical theology because of a sincere but misguided understanding of what it means to affirm the unity of Scripture's message. We suppose that if God is the author of Scripture, then it cannot contain theologies but only a theology. But while the Bible is a precious gift, inspired by God to tell us the truth about God and able to create faith in us, it is not a simple book. It tells us the truth, but it does so by using many different voices, and those voices don't always harmonize perfectly. Kenton Sparks says it well: "At face value, Scripture does not seem to furnish us with one divine theology; it gives us numerous theologies. . . . The Bible does not offer a single, well-integrated univocal theology; it offers instead numerous overlapping but nonetheless distinctive theologies!"

In other words, Scripture is unified in its message, but that unity reads more like a polyphonic novel than a systematic theology. It sounds like a riotous chorus of voices, arranged to augment and alter each other in a motley symphony, whose coherence transcends a quick listen, and not like a single voice, formally pontificating theological bullet points. As such, the unity of Scripture is not always easily explained, and certain tensions (like the ways Scripture makes sense of evil) will remain indefinitely. And when we claim the Bible *clearly* teaches something that has been rigorously debated by the best and most faithful minds for thousands of years, we could at least have the decency to blush. A couple thousand years of mercurial biblical interpretation suggest we're not being very honest with ourselves.

To this point, I think we can all agree that God was perfectly capable of producing a Bible with absolute clarity, singularity, and obviousness in relation to any and every matter under the sun, making things so divinely plain that no interpretation would be needed on our part. But that is not the Bible God has given us, presumably because God welcomes our interpretation, knowing it serves the greater mission of God, creating a people who humbly but assertively employ our hearts and minds in the quintessentially human work of knowing and loving the divine.

And once we've come clean and accepted that, it's time to roll up our sleeves and make some decisions. We will use different methods and come to different conclusions. Some will pile up the proof texts on opposing sides and weigh them in terms of quantity. Some will ask which big story can better accommodate the other big story. Some will poke and prod with theology and philosophy. Some will look at church history. I do all of the above, but then—following what I consider to be the best of classical Christian biblical interpretation throughout history—I look to Christ. Jesus is lightning, and everything else (theology, philosophy, etc.) is thunder—echoes of an event, a happening, a person. And when the echoes bring me back to their source, something becomes clear. As Hart says,

> If it is from Christ that we are to learn how God relates himself to sin, suffering, evil, and death, it would seem that he provides us little evidence of anything other than a regal, relentless, and miraculous enmity: sin he forgives, suffering he heals, evil he casts out, and death he conquers. And absolutely nowhere does Christ act as if any of these things are part of the eternal work or purposes of God. Which is well to remember.

Indeed it is. And when forced to make some kind of sense of the mystery of evil, I will always opt for whatever makes most sense in light of the life, death, and resurrection of Jesus. And Jesus never looks for the hidden hand of God in suffering nor counsels that God is the secret architect of evil. Rather, every single time Jesus confronts sickness, suffering, and death, he conquers them. Jesus reveals God as evil's destroyer and not its cloaked designer.

I know people who have lost a child and find great comfort in the belief that God ordained their child's death for his glory. I know people who have lost a child and find great comfort in the belief that God did not ordain and is not glorified by the death of their child, but hates death with a passion so fierce that he was willing to die to put death to death. Two sons fall from mountains and their fathers find solace in different things. Christ have mercy on us all. But I will go on believing and telling the story of evil, freedom, and the love of God.

Does this leave me with a boring, blank, white page? With a world of kittens and no lions?

No.

But before I explain why, I would be remiss if I failed to mention the morbid dilemma we face when evil becomes the mandatory foil to our experiencing the full range of God's glory; namely, evil (not to mention creation) becomes necessary. Because if God is equal portions love and wrath (among other attributes) and is not fully "glorified" unless all his attributes are fully expressed and actualized, then it seems God must create. In order for wrath to be expressed, there must be something other than God. And a God who *has* to create in order to become complete (or fully glorified) is not the God of orthodox Christian faith. (John 9:3 is often cited in favor of the notion that God causes evil in order to get glory from it. It can be read that way. However it does not have to be read that way. The Greek can also read "[He was born blind] let the works of God be displayed in him." In favor of the latter reading, in which Jesus negates the disciples desire to find a specific divine cause behind suffering, is Luke 13, wherein Jesus does the same thing.)

Or perhaps we want to hedge a bit and claim that while God does not need to express his wrath, we need to experience it—that evil is not of metaphysical necessity for God but epistemic necessity for us. One wonders how much that solves, considering, in this view, evil is still necessary for God's creatures to fully experience the fullness of divine glory, and God needs people to eternally torment or existentially terminate if we are to fully understand the divine nature.

So while some find a certain pastoral comfort in the idea that we need hell to properly appreciate heaven (or something to that effect), it's an idea laced with catastrophic consequences. This is not to mention the troubling picture it conjures up of God—ordaining the world be set ablaze by sin and evil so he can then play the hero by rescuing some while letting others burn because, according to a strange sense of divine justice, they deserve it. All theological constructs have their aesthetic dilemmas, but this one is especially troubling. One can argue the story of God's ordaining any and all evil for his glory is *a* biblical option—arguing that it is beautiful is quite another matter.

And this brings me back to why a blank white page is not a blank white page.

GOD IS LIGHT

Pure white light contains every color in the spectrum. Red, orange, yellow, green, blue, purple—they're all there, even though we don't have the eyes to see them without a bit of help. "God," says the writer of 1 John, "is Light, and in Him there is no darkness at all" (1 John 1:5).

So as hard as it might be for us to imagine, God's beauty does not take the form of contrasting lights and darks, charity and terror, love and wrath, but rather a boundlessly unfolding avalanche of light, charity, and love. God does not possess a plurality of variously contrasting attributes but rather the simple, everlasting, primordial generosity that we call love: "Every good thing given and every perfect gift is from above, coming down from the Father of lights, with whom there is no variation or shifting shadow" (James 1:17).

Love is "not merely one divine property *juxtaposed* to others." Love is the sole divine moral property and all God does is an expression of love. We might experience love as wrath, jealousy, and anger when we live against the grain of the universe (an idea to be returned to later), but these are not "attributes" that God "possesses." So we can claim God is wrathful and just, but only when we understand that wrath and justice are expressions of love and not independent virtues or attributes existing alongside love, providing God with a "balanced" personality. God is not "balanced." God is love. God is light and in him there is no darkness at all.

So while fallen creation is a juxtaposition of light and dark, charity and terror, love and wrath, God is not. There will be no darkness, terror, or wrath in the kingdom of God. And yet far from being a blank, boring, white page, the kingdom of God is and will be a shimmering canvas of pure white light, filled with every color. And yes, there will be lions. They will befriend baby lambs and eat straw. I have it on Isaiah's authority (Isaiah 11:6-9). If all that sounds boring, then perhaps we are boring.

Midway through the writing of this chapter, some of our dearest friends lost their baby. His name was Everett. They asked me to officiate his funeral and as I prepared, I was reminded of another funeral for a baby that I had attended years earlier. Like Everett Koop, the latter child's parents found comfort in believing God had ordained all of this for his glory, in seeing their child's death as a necessary contribution toward God's full glorification.

And while I would never begrudge anyone whatever comfort they can find in such times, I, for one, can imagine no comfort greater "than the happy knowledge that when I see the death of a child, I do not see the face of God but the face of his enemy."

I am grateful God bends even the most vile events toward his good ends (Romans 8:28), but I am far more grateful that God does not bend things in order to get glory from setting them straight.

I am grateful that while evil *is*, it was not a necessary step in a mysterious divine equation that factors out to glory—that one day it will be no more.

I am grateful the tears of children are not mandatory building blocks for the kingdom of God.

I am grateful no child will stand before Jesus and learn how her tears were required for his glory.

I am grateful Jesus will simply wipe the tears away.

His parents agreed, and asked me to say that. We ended his funeral with these words:

> While we accept Everett's death, we don't surrender to it. No—we rebel against it. We look forward to the day when God will wipe away our tears and put death to death. We don't search for hidden, divine meanings—as if the Jesus who welcomed children into his lap would take our children from us in order to teach us some "spiritual" lesson. God is light and in him there is no darkness at all. None.
>
> Our questions will remain, and we'll always wonder why, but our comfort is found in Jesus—in a God of infinite beauty and

grace, in a kingdom of light and love. So while our hearts are broken, the fire of hope still burns beneath the ashes because once you've experienced the love of Jesus, hope is a difficult fire to put out.

And so, Everett, we'll miss you, and there's a void in the world where you were supposed to be, but we won't say goodbye—because we'll see you again. The cross and resurrection of Jesus tell us so. That's our story and we're sticking to it. Thanks be to God.

SURRENDER . . . AND REBELLION

I'm soberly aware there are holes in my feeble offering toward better making sense of evil, but this seems appropriate. I do not know how to explain exactly where evil comes from. It is inexplicable, surd, horrendous. I do not understand how or why God tolerates so much evil. So by the Spirit, I wave the white flag, live the mystery, follow Christ, and trust God with the future. As Moltmann has suggested, when the dust settles, eschatology is perhaps the only credible theodicy, and we all live with holes in our theologies and hearts that only the resurrection can heal:

> No one can answer the theodicy question in this world, and no one can get rid of it. Life in this world means living with this open question, and seeking the future in which the desire for God will be fulfilled, suffering will be overcome, and what has lost will be restored. . . . It is a practical question which will only be answered through the experience of the new world in which "God will wipe away every tear from their eyes."

Saint Paul agrees: "For I consider that the sufferings of this present time are not worthy to be compared with the glory that is to be revealed to us" (Romans 8:18).

Earlier, I mentioned a word: *surrender*. And while we must surrender to evil in the sense that we should reject any and all attempts at "understanding" it by downplaying its true horror, surrender is not all that is asked of us. No—we are also taught to *rebel* against evil.

As opposed to some Eastern religions where detached surrender is the proper posture toward the world and its evil, Christianity is marked by a foundational tension between surrender and rebellion. And when this tension threatens to rip us apart, we pray, we sing, we partake of the body and blood of Christ that was pulled apart at the seams to gather us all together. We surrender, and we rebel. We shed tears, but they are buoyant tears, filled with hope, surrender, and defiance—tears that incite a resurrected rebellion, for the sake of creation, in the name of Christ. Easter doesn't make us pushovers; it makes us rebels.

CHAPTER SIX

SILENCE

BELIEVING WHEN GOD ISN'T SPEAKING

*J*n Matthew 27, Jesus hangs on the cross. He's mocked and abused, and the whole scene is unbearably cruel, but the cruelest irony of all is that he is so alone. The one sent to gather the whole world into a community of love hangs on the cross and he hangs all alone.

His closest friends have betrayed him. Strangers walking by him and hanging beside him taunt him. Then for three hours, clouds cover the sun and a deep darkness falls. For three hours Jesus hangs on the cross, abandoned, in the dark. Finally, he ruptures the silence: "My God, my God, why have you forsaken Me?" (Matthew 27:46).

It's one of the most analyzed questions in history. What does it mean? What is Jesus experiencing? What is he really asking? Clearly, Jesus is not asking why God has failed to save him. He knows he must drink the cup; he knows there's no escaping that cross alive. Rather, instead of asking why God has failed to save him, he's asking why God has forsaken him. He's asking why, in a moment of heinous cruelty, God is so silent. My God, my God—in my darkest hour, in the moment when I most need the smallest whisper—why are you so silent?

I know this question.

There was a time when I always asked God to save me. When something difficult happened, I asked God to pluck me out of the fire and pull me out of the mire and set my feet on safe, solid ground.

And that's a good, biblical prayer—God likes saving us. But I've learned that God has not promised to always save me. I understand that, instead, God has promised to always be with me. I understand there's no getting out of life alive. So I've accepted these facts and no longer always ask God to save me or save others. Now, I always ask God to be with me and with others.

My grandfather died recently, and along the way I prayed many prayers for him. But at a certain point, I stopped always asking God to save him and started asking God to be with him. Don't get me wrong—I wanted my grandfather to live to three hundred (sounded fair to me), but I understood he had lived a wonderful life, filled with love, and that life was now ending. So my prayer was that God would walk with him all the way to the end that is a new beginning.

Knowing we share this inevitable terminus, many of us have stopped expecting God to always save us. We're not greedy. We're not asking to get out of life alive. No—we're just asking God to be with us, to give us strength and courage. We're asking for the smallest whisper, the smallest hint, the smallest touch, the smallest reminder that though we walk through the valley of the shadow of death, God is with us, so we need not be afraid.

So what do we do when we look up into the heavens, only asking for a whisper, and all we hear is silence?

Why do You stand afar off, O Lord?
Why do You hide Yourself in times of trouble? (Psalm 10:1)

You, O Lord, rule forever;
Your throne is from generation to generation.
Why do You forget us forever?
Why do You forsake us so long? (Lamentations 5:19-20)

I can endure the pain and the suffering and the relentless specter of evil, but the one thing I *cannot* endure for long is the godforsaken silence. Because there comes a point at which reality is too much to bear and faith becomes nonsense if God cannot be bothered to be mindful enough of our frail frame to do something, anything really, to remind us he is there and with us and for us.

SILENCE

Years ago in a class, I was forced to read a novel (obscure at the time, but no longer since it was made into a movie) by an author whose name I could not pronounce. Procrastination had entrapped me, and I picked up the book and began reading it under a severe time crunch, expecting to skim it enough to fake my way through a class discussion. Seven hours later, I read the last sentence, closed the book, and exhaled for the first time since reading the first sentence. It remains the most moving novel I have ever read.

Silence by Shusaku Endo tells the story of a young Jesuit missionary sent to seventeenth-century Japan during a time of intense persecution for Christians. Rumor has it the young Jesuit's mentor has apostatized, so he travels to Japan in search of the truth. The truth proves elusive and along the way we are confronted with the nagging problem of the silence of God. One scene in particular captures the chill when God is silent.

Two poor, peasant Japanese Christians are discovered and sentenced to death. In order to dissuade others from becoming Christians, the authorities make a spectacle of them, tying them to wooden crosses at the edge of the ocean. When the tide rises, the frigid water creeps chin-high—just high enough to ensure a slow death. For two days they hang alone, shivering, crying out, as the inky ocean advances and retreats. Finally, they die.

His whole life this young Jesuit has been told how glorious it is
to die for your faith: "I had long read about martyrdom in the lives
of the saints—how the souls of the martyrs had gone home to Heaven,
how they had been filled with glory in Paradise, how the angels had
blown trumpets. This was the splendid martyrdom I had often seen
in my dreams."

But while dreams are pliable, reality is stiff, and as he watches two
peasants swallowed up by the sea, no angels blare heavenly trumpets.
There is nothing. There is silence:

> The martyrdom of the Japanese Christians I now describe to
> you was no such glorious thing. What a miserable and painful
> business it was! The rain falls unceasingly on the sea. And the
> sea which killed them surges on uncannily—in silence. . . .
> What do I want to say? I myself do not quite understand. Only
> that today, when for the glory of God Mokichi and Ichizo
> moaned, suffered and died, I cannot bear the monotonous
> sound of the dark sea gnawing at the shore. Behind the de-
> pressing silence of this sea, the silence of God . . . the feeling
> that while men raise their voices in anguish God remains with
> folded arms, silent.

I have seen a saint breathe his last breath, and it was not glorious.
I heard no trumpets. It was miserable, and I heard nothing. According
to the psalmist, "Precious in the sight of the LORD is the death of
His godly ones" (Psalm 116:15). Be that as it may, I cannot always
catch a view of things from behind the eyes of God, and if you've
ever watched a human die, then your romantic notions of angels and
trumpets have likely been buried beneath the miserable, painful
business of death. But if you won't take it from me (or a fictional
Jesuit missionary), perhaps you'll take it from a saint.

Most know Mother Teresa as a rock of faith who spent her entire life serving the poorest of the poor in the slums of Calcutta; that is all true, but it's not all the truth. For much of her adult life, she dealt with terrible spiritual darkness and depression. Her private letters reveal a saint of stunning light and blinding darkness:

> Darkness is such that I really do not see—neither with my mind nor with my reason.—The place of God in my soul is blank.— There is no God in me.—When the pain of longing is so great—I just long & long for God—and then it is that I feel—He does not want me—He is not there.—Heaven—souls—why these are just words—which mean nothing to me.—My very life seems so contradictory. I help souls—to go where?—Why all this? Where is the soul in my very being? God does not want me.— Sometimes—I just hear my own heart cry out—"My God" and nothing else comes.—The torture and pain I can't explain.— From my childhood I have had a most tender love for Jesus . . . but this too has gone.—I feel nothing before Jesus. . . . You see, Father, the contradiction in my life. I long for God—I want to love Him—to love Him much . . . and yet there is but pain— longing and no love.

Mother Teresa was most certainly a saint, but she was a saint who knew what it was like to take a long walk alone in the dark. Because that's what faith is at times, even for saints.

I am not much of a saint, but I am a pastor. And sometimes I have a gnawing, resentful sense that I am pouring my heart out, trying to convince people of the truthfulness of the faith, all because God cannot be bothered to say the smallest word on his own behalf. I feel like I am doing for God what God refuses to do for himself.

And so, God, why do you hide yourself in times of trouble? Why do your rod and staff not always comfort us as we walk through the valley of the shadow of death? To be clear, God, we're not asking to get out of life alive—we're just asking why you don't do more than the nothing you often seem to be doing when we need you the most. Why are you so silent?

This might be a question we must learn to live with instead of answer, so here are two thoughts that have helped me live with it a bit more faithfully.

NEGATIVITY BIAS

Trait negativity bias refers to a human tendency "to pay more attention and place more value on negative information than positive information." It means our brains are literally wired to focus on negative things instead of positive things, that "negative information weighs more heavily on the brain." It makes sense from an evolutionary perspective (no need to pay much attention to the neighbor who likes you when the real threat to your survival is the neighbor who despises you), and it is quite obviously true.

Why can a billion bits of good news fail to move your pulse a beat but a single bit of bad news send it racing? Trait negativity bias. Why can one poor interaction with someone outweigh a hundred favorable interactions? Trait negativity bias. Why can one jerk ruin the party for everyone else? Trait negativity bias. Why do you forget the thirty sermons you loved but will never, ever forget that one sermon you really disagreed with? Trait negativity bias.

I know you don't mean to, but you don't have to mean to. We do it intuitively, subconsciously. It's a reflex.

When I was twenty-three, I was the camp pastor at a summer youth camp in North Carolina. It was a great summer and one of my favorite parts of each session was receiving feedback from the youth pastors and leaders during our end-of-session evaluations. Like most humans I know, I like it when people say nice things about me, so I enjoyed reading through the evaluations and hearing how good a job I had done. But a reckoning was in route.

A group showed up, and we did not get along. These things happen from time to time, and it's nobody's fault. Chalk it up to different upbringings or personalities; you weren't meant to be best friends, so just try to be civil. We tried but failed and so by the end of the week a mutual hostility had emerged, and they let me have it in my end-of-session evaluation. The length of their list of grievances was surpassed only by its creativity.

One felt my sermons were too long.

One felt my sermons were too short.

One felt I was too arrogant. (Fair enough. I was twenty-three.)

One said I had egregiously indulged my ego and inflicted an intolerable burden on the students by inviting them to say "howdy" to me whenever they saw me. (New Yorkers don't find Texas charm very charming.)

One said he hated my accent.

One said she couldn't quite put her finger on it, but she just found me unlikable.

Had I been arrogant? Absolutely. Dead to rights. But the level of venom was so petty that I knew it shouldn't bother me. So I kept a strong, straight face as we finished the evaluations, confidently strolled back to my room, closed the door, and immediately fell into a pit of existential despair, questioning everything I thought I knew about God and my place in the universe.

"They're right. I'm the worst person in the world. I simultaneously preach too long and not long enough. I must develop a different accent. Everybody except my mother hates me. Wait—does my mother hate me?"

I know this trite misfortune should not have crushed me, and I hate that I even remember this story, but to this day I cannot remember a single one of the positive evaluations I received that summer, although I can remember every single word of the one negative evaluation.

My church recently endured a painful season of loss, and at a staff meeting we took time to talk through it—marriages that were lost or lapsing, children who were sick, children who had died. And as we sat with it all, a heavy sadness weighed on the room, and there was an unspoken sense of *why*—why wasn't God doing more; why wasn't God helping more; why was God so silent?

Eventually, someone said something: "These broken marriages and sick children are very sad, but as we mourn them we can't forget all the healthy marriages and all the healthy children." And it was like a light switched on, because while the sadness was still sad and real, we were reminded that even in midnight hours, God had done so much for us. We have so many healthy marriages, and so many healthy children, and so many children who are not healthy, but they are showered with love, and so many marriages that are limping along, but people are pushing through with moxie and forgiveness.

But we have a troubling tendency to take all the good things for granted. We feel entitled to them. We obsess over why bad things happen but rarely wonder why good things happen. Our sense of entitlement makes it hard to remember the universe does not owe us good things any more than it owes us bad things. Some of this is our faith's fault. Its breathtaking promises of eternal light and love heighten our awareness of bad things to the point that we often forget light and love are not our due. They are a gift.

All of this to say, why is God so silent sometimes? Why doesn't God do more? Perhaps God isn't silent but is doing something, yet we lack the ears to hear and the eyes to see. A loved one dies and we wonder why God did nothing. A loved one gets better and we're grateful the medicine worked. I don't think God needs us to conjure up excuses for him, but I imagine being God comes with its own divine set of problems—being blamed for every perceived failure to act but never much thanked for the billions of unforeseen mercies that sustain every single thing, every single day, sun up to sun down.

My wife went through a difficult season of doubt a couple of years ago, and in a moment of poignant honesty blurted out, "Why would I pray about this when God has never answered a single prayer of mine?" Having asked it numerous times myself, I was very sympathetic to her question, so we talked about it a bit. Could she think of a single answered prayer?

Well, there was her brother. For a couple of years we had prayed for him—that he'd find a wife who would love him for who he is but help ground him; that his infectious love for life could be channeled into a vibrant love for others. And now he was engaged to a wonderful woman who loved him dearly but was strong enough to set him straight when need be, and he had become remarkably more responsible and attentive to the needs of those around him. Was this an answered prayer or just a coincidence?

I suppose the rather obvious answer is that it could be either, and such is the case with every single attempt to document an "answered prayer." God could be doing many things, or God could be doing nothing, and yet it would all look about the same to us because our eyes target and our ears are tuned in to the tragic. He who has ears, let him hear.

That's my first thought; here's my second.

GOD, ME, WYATT

In Matthew 7:7-11, Jesus compares us to children and God to a good father, the point being that if even human parents desire to give their children what is good, how much more does God? This got me to thinking.

I am far from a perfect father, but I love my little boy, and there's not one good thing in this world I would willingly withhold from him. If it's good, I want it for him. But believe it or not, that is not always entirely clear to my son.

Last week, I took him to the park. It was a beautiful day and one of those moments I'd often looked forward to before he was born—a dad and his boy and a leisurely morning spent cavorting and getting into trouble together. Like most small boys, my son loves playing with a basketball, so we brought one along.

My eighteen-month-old son knows how to say *please*. He knows that when he wants something, he needs to say *please*.

When we arrive at the park, he runs around smiling from ear to ear, and I start dribbling the basketball on the court. This gets his attention, and he scurries over and tries to grab the ball. I gently remind him that if he wants the ball, he needs to say please. This makes him want the ball even more, so he franticly babbles, "Ball, ball, ball!" I hold on to the ball and ask him to say please. He composes himself and once again says, "Ball." Stubborn boy, but he comes by it honestly, so I say, "Wyatt, I know you want this ball, and I want to give you this ball, but you have to say *please* first."

And my eighteen-month-old son looks me in the eyes, sticks his eighteen-month-old finger in my chest and says, "Ball." Gauntlet thrown.

So I scoop up the basketball and say, "No please; no ball." And he furrows his little brow, screams at the top of his little lungs, and marches his stubborn little butt to the farthest corner of the park where he stares daggers at me for the next thirty minutes. I had a thirty-minute standoff with my toddler over please and a basketball.

I trust it goes without saying that I wanted to give him the basketball. Nothing would have made me happier. But I also wanted him to learn to say *please*, to learn to receive things instead of always taking things. All of this is perfectly clear to me, and I expect to you too, but it is not to my son. His little eighteen-month-old brain cannot understand Dad's obscure moral teleology.

And I think we can all agree that the difference between God and me is at least as great as the difference between Wyatt and me, that the cognitive gap between the creator of spacetime and a thirty-year-old dad is at least as vast as the chasm between a thirty-year-old dad and his eighteen-month-old son (go ahead, agree; it won't hurt my feelings). So if my son cannot begin to comprehend some of my ways (and I lack a single created universe to my credit), why should I think I can even begin to comprehend all of God's ways?

I understand this might sound like an artful dodge, but given our terms, I think I'm playing fair and am making a rather bare logical observation. Because if there is a God who is the maker and sustainer of this wild ride we call existence, then it makes sense that much of life will not make sense to us. I realize I'm begging the question a bit, but sometimes you have to so you can get into the question and see what things look like from the inside. And while we are perfectly free to register our complaints with the authorities, it's tough to see where we could possibly get the leverage needed to pry God off the throne and place ourselves on it. Such is the life of an ant on a rollercoaster.

God knows our pain is real, and the godforsaken silence can be deafening. God knows it can be too much sometimes, and God bless those who can't hang on long enough to see the light at the end of the tunnel is redemption instead of a train.

My God, my God—why the silence when all I'm asking for is a whisper?

You are neither the first nor the last to ask it, and as Mother Teresa said, sometimes all you can do is ask it and then "stand like a very small child and wait patiently for the storm to subside." And as you ask and wait, Christ waits with you. Christ hangs with you. Because if there's anyone who knows what it's like to feel forsaken by God, it's Christ.

*There are these two young fish swimming along, and they
happen to meet an older fish swimming the other way, who nods
at them and says, "Morning, boys, how's the water?" And the
two young fish swim on for a bit, and then eventually one of
them looks over at the other and goes, "What the hell is water?"*

DAVID FOSTER WALLACE, "THIS IS WATER"

*D*avid Foster Wallace's clever parable reminds us we have a
devilish time seeing the things closest to us, understanding
the waters we swim in. So how do you talk to a fish about water?

With the occasional caught-and-released exception, a fish does not
and cannot believe in water. There is no such thing as water. There
is the aquatic stuff in which it lives and moves and swims and has
its being, but there is no water because it has never known anything
except water.

I live and move and have always had my being in a predominantly
evangelical context—Baptist, Methodist, and nondenominational, with
a little Episcopal mixed in. I'm grateful for it in many ways—too many
to count. But as I confront my doubts and help others do the same,
three things have become clear. Evangelicalism (in many of its current
expressions) is deeply influenced by fundamentalism. Fundamentalism
is a sneaky but very serious threat to Christian faith. Talking to evangelicals about fundamentalism is like talking to a fish about water.

Earlier, I mentioned a young man who walked away from faith because he couldn't convince himself to take the early chapters of Genesis literally. I still meet with him from time to time and something has become clear: he did not reject Christianity; he rejected fundamentalism. Sadly, while that distinction could have saved his faith, it was not a distinction he could make, and he continues to struggle with it. Our mental habits run deep.

Of course he's not alone—I fear many who think they have rejected Christianity have merely rejected fundamentalism masquerading as Christianity. Helping people understand the difference (that is, trying to talk to a fish about water) is terribly difficult because fundamentalism isn't a collection of beliefs so much as it is a way of thinking, and most of us are much more equipped to discuss *what* we think than we are *how* we think. But let's define our terms. What is *fundamentalism*?

Fundamentalism proper refers to religious movements that claim to represent a return to "the fundamentals" of a given faith (one example would be the evangelical fundamentalist movement of the late 1800s and early 1900s). And while this is the *form* fundamentalism takes, fundamentalism is really more *spirit* than form; it's less a matter of specific beliefs and more a matter of general temperament. And the spirit of fundamentalism is perhaps best described as a rigid mental attitude that seeks control by pursuing certainty. It makes sense of the world by dividing things up into simple, stark categories. It is heavy on black and white and light on grey. While fundamentalism claims to be concerned with truth, one cannot help but sense it is more concerned with what "feels" certain. It will typically choose two-dimensional felt certitude over three-dimensional truth.

The basic pathology of fundamentalism is the quest for control, a quest secured through certainty, a certainty secured through a designated method of knowledge that, fundamentalism alleges, infallibly produces the whole truth and nothing but it. Instead of moving from "here is the evidence" to "this could be the truth," it moves from "I must be certain" to "this must be true." Fundamentalism mistakenly assumes it looks on the world with "a view from nowhere," objectively staring down at reality from above. And as will become clear in the following chapters, fundamentalism is equally at home on "the right" or "the left."

THE SCANDAL OF THE EVANGELICAL MIND

Mark Noll's bombshell *The Scandal of the Evangelical Mind* meticulously lays out the gradual process by which fundamentalist habits of mind came to dominate evangelical thinking in the nineteenth and twentieth centuries. It was a combination of crude Bible-only-ism, Baconian scientific method, Scottish common-sense rationalism, and an understandable but misguided rebellion against the intellectual imperialism of the rising secularism. For a fuller explanation of what all this means and how it all came together, you have to read Noll, but here's the bottom line.

In a truly novel development in the history of Christian theology, many Christians began trying to read all the Bible as literally as possible, thinking that by doing so and using the objective, fact-finding method of modern science, they could work to a sure, certain faith— the whole truth and nothing but it. Reading the Bible "literally" and "scientifically," Christians could discover truth every bit as objective as the truths being discovered in the natural sciences. And so a house of cards was built on a foundation of sand.

Because the charges are so serious, it's worth citing a number of evangelical leaders who, with the purest of intentions, built up the house of cards on the foundation of sand that is the "intellectual disaster of fundamentalism."

The great Presbyterian theologian Charles Hodge (1797–1878) said, "The Bible is to the theologian what nature is to the man of science. It is his storehouse of facts; and his method of ascertaining what the Bible teaches, is the same as that which the natural philosopher adopts to ascertain what nature teaches."

Southern Presbyterian Robert Breckenridge said theology derived from the Bible was as objective and scientific as basic geometry.

James Lamar said, "The Scriptures admit of being studied and expounded upon the principle of the inductive method; and . . . when thus interpreted, they speak to us in a voice as certain and unmistakable as the language of nature heard in the . . . observations of science."

R. A. Torrey claimed that when we apply the methods of modern science to the Bible, the result is a "careful, unbiased, systematic, thorough-going, inductive study and statement of Bible truth."

Lewis Sperry Chafer's definition of systematic theology is a fitting synthesis: "Systematic Theology is the collecting, scientifically arranging, comparing, exhibiting, and defending of all facts from any and every source concerning God and His work. . . . Contemplation of the doctrine of human conduct belongs properly to a science which purports to discover, classify, and exhibit the great doctrines of the Bible."

Long story short, as the modern world moved toward the idea that something only counts as true if we can know it "objectively," Christianity followed suit. The only difference was that whereas science unleashed the modern, objective, empirical method of knowing on nature, Christians unleashed it on the Bible. Science had nature and

Christians had the Bible, both of which allegedly yielded certainty when properly analyzed, weighed, and systematized.

The idea was that if we believe the Bible is the truth, the whole truth, and nothing but the truth, and we read it all literally, then we can reason our way to a certain faith. The sharpest shapers and practitioners of this fundamentalist biblicism often had nuanced views that tried to account for its many problems, but as is usually the case, "it was often their weaker, more simplistic ideas that shaped the thinking of subsequent generations of evangelicals." The result is that modern fundamentalist Christianity and fundamentalist scientism simply parrot each other. In a doomed quest for certitude, one flattens out reality with the Bible and the other with "science."

FLATLAND

In 1884, an English schoolmaster named Edwin Abbott Abbott wrote a story about a two-dimensional world called Flatland, inhabited by various shapes (circles, squares, etc.). In Flatland, there is height and width but no depth—the shapes are stuck in two dimensions. But one fateful night, the main character, a Square, is visited by a Sphere from the three-dimensional world of Spaceland. The Square is dazzled and dumbfounded, and when he tries to tell his fellow Flatlanders about Spaceland and a third dimension, he is locked up.

Over the last few hundred years, what seems to have happened to a great many of us is the exact opposite. Whereas we once understood we lived and moved and had our being in an enchanted, three-dimensional world of limitless mystery and wonder, we've been duped into devolving back into Flatland. We've willingly locked ourselves up in a flat world under the pretenses that doing so would provide us control, comfort, and certainty. Science does it by rejecting all reality that cannot be measured in a beaker. Christianity does it by rigid biblical literalism.

After a sermon in which I mentioned that the two creation stories of Genesis cannot both be read literally, I was confronted by a well-meaning parishioner who informed me that he had been informed the Bible was the literal word of God and any belief otherwise was a slippery slope toward perdition. He was a very kind man and had only recently become a Christian, so I understood his concerns and asked him if he had read Psalms. He had. Then I asked if he thought Psalms was the word of God. He did. Then I asked him if he read all of the psalms literally—did he believe mountains pulled up their britches and skipped along like rams when God came walking by (Psalm 114)? He assured me he did not because that would be silly. "So," I asked, "you think something can be true and the word of God and yet not literal?" A smile crept across his face and he responded, "Well—I guess I do." And intuitively, we all do.

Like many others, I read *The Chronicles of Narnia* when I was a child and it never occurred to me that Narnia was a real place and Aslan a real lion. I knew they were fictional. And yet I also knew those fictional tales of Narnia told the truth—the truth about good and evil and courage and sacrifice. In fact, I knew those fictional tales told deeper and truer truth than the "just the facts" information collected in my textbooks.

Something does not have to be literal in order to be true. In fact, the truest things probably cannot be spoken literally. Most Christians throughout history understood this and only recently "a significant minority of believers became convinced that the truth of their faith depended upon an absolutely literal . . . interpretation of scripture, and felt compelled to stake everything on so ludicrous a wager." This misled gamble goes all in on those biblical passages that touch matters of alpha and omega—how things began and will end. Firmly against the best of orthodox biblical interpretation throughout history, countless Christians now think a literal reading of Genesis and Revelation is not only correct, but also a matter of essential orthodoxy:

- I believe in God the Father.
- I believe in Christ the Son.
- I believe in the Holy Spirit.
- I believe in reading the entire Bible literally (especially the first and last chapters).

This is the fundamentalist creed, and biblical flatland is part and parcel of the fundamentalist gospel. In biblical flatland, one thinks reading the Bible rightly means reading it as literally as possible. But this violates the single most important principle of good biblical interpretation: we should read as the writer intends us to read. So if the writer is writing fiction, we should read it as fiction. If the writer is writing literal history, we should read it as literal history. If the writer is writing poetry, we should read it as poetry. If the writer is writing science, we should read it as science. If the writer is writing satire, we should read it as satire. You get the idea—you honor a writer's authority by reading as the writer intends you to read.

Take a stroll through the Bible, and you encounter a lush variety of literary landscapes—the misty hills of poetry, the dizzying peaks of John's apocalypse, the darkened caves of primal history, the level plains of wisdom. Each genre of Scripture (and there are many) must be navigated differently; otherwise, we make such a racket that we mistake our clumsy trouncing for the voice of God, hearing things God has not intended to say and not hearing things God has very much intended to say.

To return again to Psalms, when the writer says the mountains pull up their britches and skip like mountain rams when God shows up, we're clearly not supposed to interpret him literally (I've never seen a mountain skip). We're supposed to interpret him metaphorically—he's using metaphorical imagery of mountains skipping to say God is big, and beautiful, and powerful. And what he's saying is true (God is big, and beautiful, and powerful), even if it's not literally true (mountains don't wear britches or skip like rams).

Or to move in the opposite direction, the Gospels clearly ask to be interpreted more literally. To use the most famous example, when we read that Christ was raised from the dead, all indications are that the writers intend to be taken literally. In 1 Corinthians 15, Paul makes it plain that if Christ is not literally, physically raised from the dead, our faith is worthless.

Then in between the clear metaphor of Psalms and literal historicity of the resurrection, we have books like Jonah and Job where it's not all that clear what genre we are reading. So we do our best, trusting that God will find a way to speak to us so long as we have ears to hear.

To reiterate: we honor the authority of God, mediated through the Bible, by doing our best to read as the writers intend us to read, not by reading as literally as possible. In many cases, reading as literally as possible is an act of misguided faithfulness that subverts the Bible's authority by flattening its wonderfully diverse landscapes into an arid desert of literalism.

SLIPPERY SLOPES

If that sounds like a slippery slope ("Once we read *some* of the Bible metaphorically, how do we keep from reading *all* of it metaphorically?"), I understand, so it's good to be reminded that we have thousands of years of careful, genre-specific interpretation to guide us. We are not setting out on virgin territory. We are treading a well-worn path staked out by our fathers and mothers in the faith. They will teach us to—humbly but confidently—interpret contextually, as the writer intends.

It also bears pointing out that the fixation on slippery slopes is typically driven by the fundamentalist desire for certainty. It's a diversionary tactic, an attempt to avoid asking, "Is this true?" by asserting, "If this is true then it will make a mess, and because messes are bad, this can't be true." And if we are still worried about slippery slopes, I would offer the anecdotal observation that I know more people who left faith because rigid biblical literalism let them down than I do those who left because they read parts of the Bible metaphorically. In other words, rigid biblical literalism can itself be a slippery slope that leads to flatland and broken faith.

The self-assured, naive, dogmatic biblicism of fundamentalism (wryly assessed by John Howard Yoder as a "form of theological culture that assumes there are no hermeneutical problems since what I take a text to mean is what it has to mean") has left many Christians intellectually crippled and terrified, spending all their time protecting every single spade, heart, diamond, and club in a towering house of cards, fearing the smallest tremor will send the whole thing crashing down. This mentality creates a culture where everything becomes a "gospel issue" because everything affects the entire thing.

(As an aside, I keep a running list of things I've been told are gospel issues—a list that currently includes, but is not limited to rapture, evolution, inerrancy, women [not] speaking in church, double imputation, speaking in tongues, not speaking in tongues, alcohol, eternal conscious torment, and Harry Potter. From this I have gathered the gospel message is something along these lines: "Ask Jesus into

your heart by believing in double imputation so you can be taken in
the rapture, unless you speak in tongues (or don't speak in tongues),
or drink alcohol, or believe in evolution, or let women speak in
church, or don't believe in inerrancy or eternal conscious torment,
or enjoyed reading Harry Potter.")

Fundamentalism never tires of drawing narrower lines in the sand
and giving us more ways to lose our faith.

In summing up his devastating critique of evangelical fundamentalism, Mark Noll likens it to cancer treatment. Faced with the threat
of a growing, aggressive secularization of knowledge, evangelical
fundamentalism did what it thought it had do to survive, and in
some sense, it succeeded. And yet the version of Christianity that
survived has been horribly disfigured by the cure itself. Specifically,
fundamentalism's naive confidence in its ability to glean the objective
facts of the Bible through its "plain" reading method left many Christians unable to handle the challenges posed by Darwinianism and
higher biblical criticism. We still suffer the fallout. Fundamentalism
has its virtues; thinking is not one of them. Love the fundamentalist;
hate the fundamentalism.

Flatland also has its virtues—among them, simplicity and a spine.
I can appreciate both, and not everything in the world is grey. But
we do not live in flatland, and the Bible has a depth that violates all
two-dimensional readings. This is not a bad thing—it means the
Bible expresses reality. As evangelical biblical scholar Gordon Fee
puts it:

> God did not choose to give us a series of timeless, non-culture-
> bound theological propositions to be believed and imperatives
> to be obeyed. Rather, he chose to speak his eternal Word *this*
> way, in historically particular circumstances and in every kind

of literary genre. By the very way God gave us this Word, he locked in the ambiguity.

What is true of the Bible is true of reality at large: the ambiguity is locked in. Embrace it. Celebrate it! And please remember that a flat world painted black and white is not your only alternative to a hopelessly uneven world painted grey. Our faith boasts a long line of graffiti artists eager to show us creatively faithful ways forward.

*A*s a pastor, I try to keep tabs on the temperature in the room. It comes in handy when trying to speak the truth in love. You need to know where people are and what they can handle; otherwise, you might shine too much well-intentioned light in their eyes and they will leave blinded instead of enlightened. When avoidable, we should not lose our influence just so we can make a point. On this particular Sunday, however, my pastoral thermometer failed me.

We were in the last week of a series in which we had tackled very thorny questions, and we were wrapping things up with a Q&A. I was asked a question about evolution and, as it would turn out, far too cavalierly answered that I saw no necessary incompatibility between evolution and Christian faith. I opened my inbox on Monday and discovered that in addition to having come across condescendingly, I had also done a terrible job explaining myself.

I'm a perfectionist by nature, so my initial response to criticism is to challenge you to a duel for daring to suggest I did something imperfectly. But once I get over myself (and sometimes it takes a while), I want to learn from my mistake. So after taking a few days and writing a few incredibly juvenile responses that, mercifully, never saw the light of day, I tried to understand how and why I had handled that question so poorly. And I was reminded of an event from my father's childhood.

He was in a Sunday school class, listening to his teacher expound on Genesis 1 and a young earth, and asked his teacher how to make sense of all those dinosaur bones. "Was there no room for Rex on the ark?" he asked, with guileless sincerity. "The devil buried the bones," his teacher answered, and proceeded to explain that a literal Genesis 1 and young earth were essential to Christian faith. My father found himself before a fork in the road. There he was, a young boy who loved Jesus and dinosaurs, and the die had been cast—either the Prince of Darkness had spent the better part of the last millennia burying dinosaur bones or there was no God.

This is the kind of baggage many of us, myself included, have been forced to carry into conversations about faith and science.

Strange things happen in war; desperate times call for desperate measures. And in the minds of many modern folks, faith is at war with science. Militant atheists and Christians march into the field, prime their muskets, and then fire away. The results are predictable—few casualties, much maiming. The wearisome squabbles produce lots of heat but little light, and the volleys of musket fire overpower the more sensible voices. The convergence of faith and science is a frontier that needs exploring, not a battlefield that needs crusading.

And surely all the crusading is partly responsible for the rather stunning revelation that, in the United States, atheists are more likely than Christians to feel a sense of wonder about the universe. Many Christians are now immune to awe when standing before starry heavens, and this immunity is perhaps blasphemy. Other faithful explorers have and will continue to do the heavy lifting, so what I offer here are a few simple thoughts guiding me as I navigate the thicket.

IS GOD DEAD?

"Science takes things apart to see how they work. Religion puts them together to see what they mean."

When dealing with something as complex as the relationship between faith (or religion) and science, a stark, simplified frame can give things some needed perspective, and Rabbi Jonathan Sacks's punchy explanation does just that. Certainly, there is more to be said and many qualifications to be made, but on the whole, I think Sacks is right: faith and science look at the world from different angles, asking primarily different questions, and when this difference is forgotten, reality's depth collapses into something flat, manageable, and banal. And when reality gets flat, manageable, and banal, it is no longer reality. Or to say this another way, people of faith and no faith often end up chasing each other in circles because both have forgotten that God does not "exist."

In April of 1966, *Time* magazine published a cover at least a couple hundred years in the making. The background is black, the letters are red, and the question is brass: Is God dead? Many people think so. Here's the story they tell.

Long ago primitive people invented religion to explain events they could not understand. A Neanderthal sees a lightning bolt flash down from the heavens, and because he doesn't understand the atmospheric sciences, he (simple Neanderthal that he is) mistakenly assumes there must be some man up in the clouds, hurling down said lightning bolts. What else could it be? This story of the man in the clouds is passed down through generations until it becomes the story of the god in the heavens—a god like Zeus. And, allegedly, all gods and religions were more or less created this way: unexplainable events, attributed to the gods.

And the gods have a good run. For thousands of years they rule the earth, and the peoples bow to them in reverent submission, but then along comes science, explaining all these previously unexplainable events, leaving deicide in its wake. No god in the heavens hurls down lightning bolts—there are just water droplets and ice crystals rubbing against each other to produce static electricity. So if Zeus was only good for causing an unexplainable physical event, and science can now explain that event, there's really no need for Zeus anymore. Zeus is simply an antiquated scientific explanation. Zeus is dead, and science has killed him. So it goes with all the gods and religions. The venerable Nietzsche says it best: "God is dead . . . and we have killed him."

Needless to say, the story of gods and religions is a bit more complicated than that, seeing as how ancient religions, while certainly including ancient science, were more concerned with axiological explanations than scientific ones. That is, they were primarily concerned with pointing to things of worth, value, and meaning. That's another story for another day, but the thing to mention here is the irony that while scientifically inclined atheists and scientifically antagonistic believers disagree about whether or not God is dead, they tend to agree on a basic premise that serves as the flawed foundation for the whole conversation: either God does something or nature does something.

For example: What created the diverse forms of life on earth? Evolution or God? Many atheists and Christians answer differently, but they agree it is a binary question, because they agree God and nature are in causal competition with one another. Some short reflections on sex and gravity reveal this is a mistake.

What created my son? Did egg and sperm join to make a zygote cell, or did my wife and I intentionally decide to make a baby? I am just old-fashioned enough to think a man is never in competition with his sperm. So, yes, egg and sperm joined to make a zygote cell and, yes, my wife and I intentionally decided to make a baby. Both explanations are true and are not competing explanations because they are different levels of explanation. They are true in different ways, but they are *both* true. Thus when the psalmist says God knit him together in his mother's womb (Psalm 139:13), he does not mean God overrode the normal biological processes that form babies in order to knit the psalmist himself; rather, he means the biological processes are how God knit him together in his mother's womb.

What upholds the planets as they dangle in empty space on their journey round the universe? God or gravity? Again—this is a silly question. Can you imagine someone refusing to believe in God because they believe in gravity?

"Why don't you believe in God? Gratuitous suffering? Metaphysical grievances? Other religions?"

"No, no. Gravity."

God and gravity are not in competition with one another. We might say gravity is how God rules the planets.

And now we come back to evolution and the unnecessary maiming it continues to cause. Although many Christians have been deceived into thinking scientists are somewhat split over the theory of evolution, this is false. Scientists are not split over evolution. Every reputable survey you come across puts scientific support for evolution in the range of 90-99 percent, with that number tending toward the latter among scientists who actually specialize in fields that would make them experts on the issue. This is a remarkable consensus. Yes, the theory itself continues to evolve and mature, but the basic premise that terrestrial life has evolved over time from common ancestry has been confirmed over and over. And God need be in competition with evolution no more than God need be in competition with sperm or gravity. There's more to say here, but first, I'll circle back to that seemingly provocative but merely ancient, essential, orthodox assertion that God does not "exist."

GOD DOES NOT "EXIST"

Yuri Gagarin was a Russian cosmonaut and the first human in space. Upon his return, Nikita Khrushchev, the premier of the Soviet Union, an atheist, mockingly quipped that Gagarin flew up into the divine, heavenly abode, and yet God was nowhere to be found. This legendary story hints at the radical flaw ruining much thinking and talking about God. Here are two statements:

- The book is on the table.
- God is in heaven.

At first glance, they might seem comparable. There are two objects that are said to exist somewhere in the universe. We can find the book on the table and prove it exists, and we can find God in heaven and prove God exists. But despite their superficial similarity, the two statements are not remotely comparable because God does not "exist" much less inhabit some physical place called heaven.

God is not a super-powerful creature, really big and strong and smart, who inhabits the universe and performs allegedly unexplainable physical events. God is not like Zeus. God does not "exist" because God is both beyond existence and is existence itself. God is not a being because God is both beyond being and is being itself. God is the infinite ocean of being that endlessly begets and sustains the wild and wondrous ride called existence. God does not live and move and have his being in the universe, but, as David Hart reminds us, the universe lives and moves and has its being in God:

> To speak of "God" properly . . . is to speak of the one infinite
> source of all that is: eternal, omniscient, omnipotent,

omnipresent, uncreated, uncaused, perfectly transcendent of all things and for that very reason absolutely immanent to all things. . . . He is not a "being" . . . he is not one more object in the inventory of things. . . . Rather, all things that exist receive their being continuously from him, who is the infinite wellspring of all that is. . . . In one sense he is "beyond being." . . . In another sense he is "being itself" . . . the unity and simplicity that underlies and sustains the diversity of finite and composite things. Infinite being, infinite consciousness, infinite bliss, from whom we are, by whom we know and are known, and in whom we find our only true consummation.

One is tempted to chastise much modern atheism for the straw-man caricatures of God it continues to burn down, but perhaps there would be fewer of these if we Christians quit defending those straw-men gods. Let them burn! One can understand how the amateur atheist could think science proves (or even has the capacity to prove) that God does not exist, but we should know better. We should know that God does not "exist." How did we forget?

That is a complicated story of theological creep, wherein the fundamental doctrine of divine transcendence was slowly and unintentionally subverted as the line between Creator and creation was blurred. In my context, this subversion of proper divine transcendence metastasized in the culture of popular, fundamentalist Christianity, a result of which is the booming cottage industry of pseudosciences that claim to definitively prove the existence of God by the physical events of the universe.

In a sincere but misled attempt to "prove" God's "existence," we have shrunk the infinite Creator of space and time into a super-powerful creature so we can look for proofs of his actions in the physical events of the universe. Instead of looking for Zeus's lightning bolts, we look for irreducible complexity or intelligent design—things that, supposedly, only God can explain. And while there might be a grain of truth in these pursuits, they miss the forest for the trees and fall back on the familiar mistake of "God of the gaps" thinking, wherein God is used to explain physical events we cannot currently explain (and as I once heard a friend say, the problem with God of the gaps is that when you run out of gaps, you run out of God). An illustration borrowed from Richard Taylor helps bring the forest back into focus.

Imagine you are wandering through the woods and come across a giant, floating, translucent sphere. Clearly, you would be astonished at the sight of it and question how on earth it came to be there, out in the middle of the woods. And you would never be able to believe it just happened to be there, without any further cause or explanation. You'd be shocked into wonder and curiosity at the sight of such a thing.

But you should feel the same shock, wonder, and curiosity at the sight of every single thing in the woods: a rock, a leaf, a tree, a squirrel. How wild and wondrous it is that anything at all should exist! The giant, floating, translucent sphere shocks us because we are not used to it. A tree does not shock us because we are used to it. But in those fleeting moments when we truly awaken to the world, we sense how ridiculous and miraculous it is that anything at all should exist. Everything is a miracle!

My son is not yet so familiar with the world to take it all for granted. His world is enchanted—everything is magic. When he sees a bird, he clumsily races toward it yelling, "Bird! Bird! Bird!" It might as well be a unicorn. When he sees a dog, time might as well stand still. Then there are the adults. We see a tree, a bird, a dog, a person, the sun, and we yawn—seen plenty of those before. But not my son. He apprehends the mystery of existence, of being itself. He remembers something most of us have long forgotten. He sees the forest *and* the trees.

So instead of bickering over whether God or evolution designed humans, or whether the complexity of the human eye is so irreducible as to be a proof for God, we would be better served walking around in wide-eyed wonder, marveling that anything and everything should exist: "That there is a world is a miracle. The question, therefore, is never 'Does God exist?' Rather, what should astonish us is that we exist." From gaping black holes in the deepest reaches of space to the tiniest pebble outside your front door, all of it is shocking because existence itself is the miracle.

The issue is not gaps that God does or does not fill in creation, but the absolute chasm between existence and nonexistence. And before this chasm, evolution, biogenesis, and physics fall silent. But back to evolution for a moment.

RED IN TOOTH AND CLAW

How does evolution challenge Christianity?

Among believers and nonbelievers, the antagonism between evolution and Christianity (and most religions) is so assumed that it is rarely explained. But in what specific ways does evolution conflict with Christianity? One could multiply alleged conflicts *ad infinitum*, but five stand out.

First, and as discussed in the previous chapter, evolution conflicts with rigid biblical literalism. If we read the first two chapters of Genesis as a literal description of how God made the world, then evolution and Christianity are in conflict. But we should not read Genesis 1 and 2 literally! In fact, a rigidly literal reading of Genesis 1 and 2, resulting in the belief that God created the world ten thousand years ago (known as young-earth creationism), has only gained traction within the last hundred years. It is an overwhelmingly minority position in orthodox Christian theology, a novelty on the theological scene. As Noll states, "Despite widespread impressions to the contrary, [young-earth] creationism was not a traditional belief of nineteenth-century conservative Protestants or even of early twentieth-century fundamentalists."

This needs to be said as clearly, consistently, and charitably as possible: not only is rigid biblical literalism and young-earth creationism not essential, but it is fundamentally biblically, theologically, philosophically, historically, and scientifically mistaken. It may come from a sincere place, but it can be very dangerous. It produces bad Bible reading, bad theology, and very bad science. Consider for a moment the following quotation:

> Calvin's doctrine of creation is, if we have understood it aright, for all except the souls of men, an evolutionary one . . . not only evolutionism but pure evolutionism. . . . And this, we say, is a very pure evolutionary scheme.

This is B. B. Warfield, a conservative Calvinist and the godfather of the Protestant doctrine of inerrancy, summarizing Calvin on creation! It boggles the mind that a very conservative, Calvinist, inerrantist Christian writing one hundred years ago could be so accepting of evolution when so many of his Protestant great-grand-children would consider belief in evolution heresy. We have strayed far from center when our theology makes someone like B. B. Warfield look "liberal."

So while evolution is in conflict with biblical literalism and young-earth creationism, a biblical literalism that *necessitates* young-earth creationism is in conflict with the best of historic, orthodox biblical interpretation, especially in regards to Genesis 1–2. Or to say it another way, most ancient interpreters, relying on ancient science, did think the world was quite young (they also thought it was quite flat). But most of the best ancient interpreters did not employ a rigid biblical literalism that *forced them* into believing the earth *had to be young* in order for Scripture to be true. Augustine believed the earth was flat and young; however, his interpretive methods make it clear that if he lived now, he would not. For example, Augustine suggests that when science *proves* something that seems to contradict Scripture, the proven scientific truth should take precedence over the literal sense of Scripture.

All this is to say that, if some Christians want to make a *scientific* argument that the earth, despite all appearances from several different scientific fields of inquiry, is only a few thousand years old, that is perfectly acceptable. What is not acceptable is Christians demanding Genesis 1–2 be read literally, and then bending, censoring, or ignoring science to make it say what a literal reading of Genesis 1–2 has already determined it has to say: namely, the earth is young.

Second, some feel evolution conflicts with the dignity of human beings, as taught by Scripture. As one of Darwin's contemporary critics put it, "Darwinism casts us all down from this elevated platform, and herds us all with four-footed beasts and creeping things. It tears the crown from our heads; it treats us as bastards and not sons, and reveals the degrading fact that man in his best estate . . . is but a civilized, dressed up, educated monkey, who has lost his tail."

Humans think highly of ourselves, so there can be an initial indignation toward the idea that we are cultured monkeys with missing posterior appendages. But really, does it matter whether we're the direct descendants of dirt a few thousand years ago (Genesis 2:7) or prehuman primates a hundred thousand years ago? Is dirt of nobler stock than a chimp? And of course, according to evolution, trace back humanity's family tree far enough and we are descendants of a cosmic explosion—the Big Bang! That is, trace back our family tree far enough, and we are stardust. Either way, we reduce to stardust, animated by the breath of God. I cannot imagine a more royal pedigree.

And think of this—if evolution is true, then we are the culmination of countless species, over millions of years, who have all left a trace of themselves in us. Ernan McMullin observes this would mean that

> when Christ took on human nature, the DNA that made him the son of Mary may have linked him to a more ancient heritage stretching far beyond Adam to the shallows of unimaginably ancient seas. And so, in the Incarnation, it would not have been just human nature that was joined to the Divine, but in a less direct but no less real sense all those myriad organisms that had unknowingly over the eons shaped the way for the coming of the human.

Count me among those who find this inspiring instead of insulting.

Third, some feel evolution conflicts with Christianity's teaching that God intervenes in creation. The God of Scripture intervenes in creation, and if evolution is a completely closed system in which God cannot or does not intervene, then evolution is in conflict with Christianity.

For me, this alleged conflict is a good deal more complicated than the first two. I do think Scripture teaches that God acts "specially" in creation and that Christianity is, literally, birthed from the special action of God in space and time—from exodus to incarnation to resurrection. And yet I think we must be careful when invoking the idea that divine intervention is in conflict with evolution. I agree with Keith Ward:

I think the word "intervention" has done a great deal of harm. . . . You do not have to think of God as a being who interferes in the clockwork of the universe to adjust the works from time to time. You could think of God as the deepest reality of the universe. . . . God does not have to intervene in a closed universe. God is the reality within which the physical universe exists, and without which the universe would not exist at all. . . . You need to get away from the idea that there is a closed set of physical laws, which do not quite manage to produce life and mind and reason by themselves, so that God has to step in to keep redirecting things to get the results God wants.

Many theologians share similar concerns, suggesting the universe contains a deep rational order, able to move toward certain goals without needing God's constant "intervention." God creates and constantly sustains the universal, rational order of creation, but does God intentionally make creation physically incomplete so he can then physically intervene? Some see problems with this idea.

Others, such as Alvin Plantinga, suggest we're really not very good at even understanding what it means for God to "intervene" and have no clue whether the universe is "closed." According to some variations of quantum mechanics, it could well be the case that God is constantly "acting specially in the world and the material universe is never causally closed." So perhaps it would be better to think that instead of occasionally intervening in creation from the outside, God constantly participates in creation from the inside: in him we live and move and have our being (see Acts 17:28).

Obviously we don't have all this anywhere near sorted out, so it seems appropriate to humbly and patiently work out what it means for God to "intervene" in creation and resist painting ourselves into unnecessary corners. At minimum, even if evolution is a completely closed system, there is no necessary conflict between that and the biblical teaching that God acts in creation. At most, it would mean God does not regularly suspend the natural laws God himself created in the process of evolution, because those divine natural laws are perfectly capable of bringing about the results God intended. If I'm pulling my son along in his little red wagon, I am equally involved in this action regardless of whether the wagon rides along perfectly or if I must occasionally inflate the wheels and tighten a few screws.

Fourth, evolution makes us fundamentally revise some traditional understandings of the fall, wherein the literal fall of a literal Adam and Eve first introduces suffering, evil, and death into the world. Science tells us the creation of humanity was not a singular, instant event involving the creation of a single human pair, Adam and Eve. Rather, it appears we evolved from a population of about 10,000 hominid ancestors that first appeared approximately 200,000 years ago. Science also tells us that suffering and death were present in the world *millions* of years before humans arrive on the scene. In light of this, how do we make sense of the fall? Perhaps something like this.

In the beginning, God created the heavens and the earth, but God did not create the heavens and the earth fully realized. God created them unfinished, full of potential and futurity. In the beginning, God created the heavens and the earth and did so in a way that allowed creation to unfold gradually. God created a creation that evolves—and evolves toward humanity—but does so very slowly.

Eventually, the process of evolution produces a population of hominids with an emerging religious awareness, a sense of the divine. A relationship, albeit an embryonic one, between God and humanity is established. We might think of this, metaphorically, as the "creation" of Adam and Eve. And at this first dawn of religious awareness and relationship, humanity is "naked but not ashamed." We might call this "Eden":

> Eden in this model represents the possibility that human beings were capable of divine recognition, but had no self-conscious evil tendencies. Before that there would have been some acts that harmed other persons, but they were more akin to that most commonly found in other animals, and therefore reactive and transactional rather than deliberate and transcendent.

Humans do things that are wrong but are not "sinful" because they lack the maturity to be held to account. They are spiritual babies (see Romans 5:13, where Paul seems to think along these lines).

However, this religious awareness eventually evolves to the point where humans are no longer spiritual babies but adults and, as adults, capable of *sin*. That is, they grow capable of deliberate rebellion against God. And once they grow capable of sin, they sin, and the power of humanity's sin is unleashed on the world. Humanity has "fallen."

This fall is historical—it is an actual phenomenon that took place in history. But it is not a single event wherein a single human pair that God made from dirt a few thousand years ago rebels against God. It is a real fall, but it is gradual, episodic, and social instead of instant, literal, and individual. Suffering and death are present in creation prior to human sin, perhaps fallout of the primal catastrophe of an angelic fall. Sin enters the world through "Adam," and sin brings with it a kind of spiritual death that spreads to all humanity (Romans 5:12). The world becomes a place where it is impossible not to be a sinner. This, I think, does what a doctrine of the fall needs to do from a biblical and theological standpoint, while still being true to the findings of modern science. And as Augustine reminded us earlier, when science proves something that *seems* to contradict Scripture, the proven scientific truth should take precedence over the literal sense of Scripture.

Fifth and finally, evolution challenges Christianity by exacerbating the problem of evil. And this was the challenge that moved Darwin himself, once an aspiring pastor, toward a troubled agnosticism later in life. Simply put, evolution is a brutal, vicious, wasteful, and cruel process. It involves the creation of life through monstrous violence over immense ages of time. It is difficult to believe the God who would use evolution to bring about humanity could be the same God who took on flesh in Christ to redeem humanity. As Philip Kitcher memorably puts it:

> When you consider the millions of years in which sentient creatures have suffered, the uncounted number of extended and agonizing deaths, it simply rings hollow to suppose that all this is needed so that, at the very tail end of history, our species can manifest the allegedly transcendent good of free and virtuous action.

And this is quite the problem. It should bother us. Though to be fair, it is not really a problem that Darwinism first posed. Tennyson observed that nature was "red in tooth and claw" before Darwin suggested our ancestors sported tails. So while Darwin perhaps accentuated things by teaching us the stunning variety of life on earth is the result of mass extinctions over millions of years, this was simply a modern scientific restatement of the ancient problem of evil, and I, for one, find evil terribly troubling regardless whether it involves mass extinctions over millions of years or the suffering of a single child. Darwin himself lost his little girl to a tragic death, and one wonders what toll this took on his belief. Evil is and remains a blasphemy you either do or don't trust God to sort out.

But God takes his time—Scripture says it, the saints accept it, and evolution confirms it. So I will wait. As I wait, I wait with agonizing questions as to why a God of infinite charity would allow a world of, seemingly, infinite cruelty. I see creativity and elegance in evolution, but I also see violence and waste. Creation is beautiful but fallen, including evolution. And while the specter of evil is ancient, perhaps we do bear a novel burden here. Perhaps our distant mothers and fathers in the faith, while no strangers to suffering, glimpsed a kinder universe thanks to their ignorance of the evolutionary process. For we, even when confronted with the simple beauty of, say, a monarch butterfly, are haunted by the knowledge that those bright, orange wings declare not just the beauty of God but the brutality of nature.

So we must be careful discerning God's purposes from within nature because while the starry heavens declare the glory of God, the crimson sod we tread tells a darker story. God has a purpose *for* nature, but this does not mean God's purposes are easily perceived *within* nature. Indeed, God's ultimate purpose for nature is glimpsed only in new creation, meaning it is only in light of the end that we can understand the beginning or the present: "the end is in the beginning."

And if we're still not convinced evolution might be compatible with Christian faith, that's okay, but perhaps some of what has been said can at least help us understand that its incompatibility has been seriously overstated, and we have some more considering to do.

And perhaps a final observation bears mentioning: God does not owe us—and has not seen fit to give us—a detailed explanation regarding the origins and mechanics of the universe. I wish that weren't so. I feel like we have enough mysteries to live with and God could have thrown us a bone here. But this is the essence of a life of faith, constantly forced to live with mysteries that are not of our own choosing.

Setting our sights in a different direction, it might be helpful to close by briefly discussing the ways in which forgetting that God does not "exist" has gotten modern science into a bit of trouble.

THE THEORY OF EVERYTHING

Science explores the physical world using physical tools. Science is good at this and we should be thankful for it. Science gets in trouble when it forgets it is exploring the physical world using physical tools and clumsily attempts to distill the whole of reality into a physical world wholly explainable using wholly physical tools. Science gets in trouble when it brashly subjects God to scientific analysis.

Because, again, God is not a creature who "exists." God is not physically observable or measurable. God cannot be placed in a beaker. Technically, it is manifestly certain that science in and of itself has little to nothing to say about God. So when you find folks saying (always very confidently) that science proves God does not exist, all they are actually saying is they do not understand God, or they do not understand science, or they do not understand either. They are woodpeckers trying to fell a redwood.

For example, suppose you shot a film in black and white, and then proceeded to use your black and white film as proof that color does not exist. "See! There is no such thing as color. Blue, green, red—they are all illusions. My film is the proof!" But of course you can't see color—your method assured that from the start.

In a similar sense, when science goes into the world, only measuring and taking into account the physically measurable and observable, it only finds the physically measurable and observable. It is ludicrous for science to then conclude, "See! There are no spiritual things. There is no God. There are only physical things." The circularity of this argument is so crude it often goes unperceived, basically boiling down to something akin to, as Hart cleverly says, "Physics explains everything, which we know because anything physics cannot explain does not exist, which we know because whatever exists must be explicable by physics, which we know because physics explains everything."

The mistake of much modern science was turning a method into a metaphysic. It set out to explain the physical processes of the world without recourse to God (method), had—properly understood—moderate success, and somehow came to the conclusion this meant there was no God (metaphysic). It forgot that the limits of scientific inquiry are by no means the limits of reality. This is quite the mistake, considering "it is certain that all possible scientific findings are compatible with the conception of a transcendent creator-God." It is certainly possible there is no God, and it is certainly impossible that science could ever tell us that. In fact, I am inclined to declare there is not a single, orthodox, classic theological claim that science has disproved.

Indeed, when science stops going à la carte and uses all its findings (in biology, physics, astronomy, etc.) to cobble together a grand theory of everything, it typically presents something amusingly theistic. Take, for example, Stephen Hawking's ambitious book *The Theory of Everything*, in which he explains the origin of the universe in terms of a quantum vacuum and quantum laws. In short, our universe is the creation of a quantum vacuum, governed by quantum laws, outside of time, that necessarily expresses the mathematical laws it holds. So the theory of everything, according to one of the smartest men ever to live, is a . . .

necessary,

eternal,

transcendent

quantum

vacuum.

I don't suppose I am the only one who suspects this is just a particularly abstruse way to say "God." I would only add that the necessary, eternal, transcendent quantum vacuum took on flesh, died for our sins, was raised on the third day, and has a personal face turned toward us in love.

So Hawking can pray or not pray to the necessary, eternal, transcendent quantum vacuum, but I feel well within my rights to pray to the God of Abraham, Isaac, and Jacob. You should too.

*F*undamentalism and science pose gravely unnecessary threats to modern Christianity. But the gravest threat to modern Christianity is neither fundamentalism nor science, but stuff. For all intents and purposes, stuff is the new religion, which brings me to the story of a sly, shrewd demon named Mammon.

"No one can serve two masters; for either he will hate the one and love the other, or he will be devoted to the one and despise the other. You cannot serve God and mammon" (Matthew 6:24 RSV).

So here is Jesus, claiming we cannot serve God and mammon, *mammon* being an Aramaic term for "wealth" or "possessions" or "stuff." Over time, the term *mammon* took on a life of its own, eventually becoming Mammon—the demon of wealth and greed. Some considered him one of the seven princes of hell, others the prince of darkness himself. And this sneaky demon devised the most deviously brilliant plan heaven or hell has ever seen.

"So how do we kill God?"

Satan poses the question, and his minions brainstorm. Of course, technically speaking, there is no *killing* God, but they know what he means: How do we kill the worship of God? The diabolical assembly is whipped into delirium as a wild menagerie of fiendish plans pours forth. They are vicious, violent, and complex. So many poisons to choose from! But in the midst of the frenzy, Mammon calmly walks to the podium and speaks softly. The crowd hushes in time to hear the crux of his plan:

"I will give them so much stuff that they won't want there to be a God."

The baser demons cackle and howl—what a ridiculous idea! Clearly a more explicit assault is needed. But a slow smile creeps across Satan's face because he knows; this is exactly how you kill God.

Modern, militant atheism has typically gone the route of trying to make God unnecessary, typically by using "science." We don't need God to explain the presence or variety of life on earth. We don't need God to explain morality. We don't need God to explain consciousness. So the claims go, and this method has been moderately effective, but only moderately, for at least two reasons. First (as discussed in the previous chapter), science, while wonderful and helpful beyond measure, is completely incapable of making God unnecessary, so long as we are actually talking about God. Second, this method appeals primarily to our reason, which is a problem because humans are far less reasonable than we give ourselves credit for.

We like to think of ourselves as "brains-on-a-stick." We calmly, coolly, rationally think our way through the world, come to the appropriate conclusions, and then choose appropriately. Our behaviors (what we do) and desires (what we want) are the result of a clean, rational process. We *think* our way to what we should want. We move from reason to desire—we reason our way to what is true and good and beautiful, and then act and desire accordingly. All of this is true except when it's not, which happens to be most of the time because humans are not the thinkers we think we are. We are lovers before we are thinkers.

So instead of impassively gliding from reason to desire, we voraciously thrash from desire to reason. We do not think our way to what we should want; we want our way to how we should think. In plainer terms, we have primal, pre-intellectual desires that have such gravity they bend our logic wherever and however they please. Better yet, our hearts simply *love* certain things and our minds produce whatever logic is needed to help us get what we love. Reason is the slave of desire.

For example, I want a jet ski. I did not reason my way to this want. I did not sit in my ivory tower, contemplate the heat of a Texas summer, and come to the logical conclusion that I should want a jet ski. Rather, I've been conditioned to associate jet skis with luxury and happiness (money cannot buy happiness, but it can buy jet skis, and jet skis make people happy), and I instinctively want luxury and happiness, so I instinctively want a jet ski. So because I want the jet ski, I will now reason my way to why it is good and right for me to want it: the heat of a Texas summer, I'll share it, and so on. Greater love hath no man than to share his jet ski.

Yes, yes—it's a bit more complicated than that, and reason and desire's relationship is not as one-way as I'm implying, but that's just to prove the point that desire influences reason every bit as much (and more) as reason influences desire. Mammon knows this, so rather than appeal to humanity's reason, Mammon seduced humanity's desire. Because if you really want to get rid of God, you don't make God unnecessary, you make God inconvenient. You entice humanity with more—more status, more stuff, more *more*— and once enticed, humanity will do the dirty work of killing the God who would challenge their insatiable desire for more. Indeed, the human desire for God runs far too deep for "science" or "reason" to ever hope to displace it. In order to cure the world of its desire for God, you need to make it desire something more than God: namely, stuff.

There are two stories to tell here. One is short, simple, and personal. The other is long, complex, and public.

FOR THE LOVE OF MONEY . . .

I know a story of a man who was once a faithful husband, dad, and church deacon. He is no longer any of those things. He cheated on his wife, abandoned his children, and left his church. No need to throw stones here—but for the grace of God go I (and you too). When asked why, he says it is because he's just not sure there is a God, vaguely referencing science, other religions, moral relativity—the usual suspects. I don't mean to patronize. Those suspects can be serious stumbling blocks. But the more of the story you know, the more skeptical you become of these reasons.

Apparently, this man is not one who agonizes over existential mysteries or reads serious books on science, other religions, or moral relativity. And as I am told it, his journey away from faith was not set in motion by doubt or skepticism or reason or a flash of transcendent empathy, but by a windfall of cold, hard cash. Overnight, his company became hugely successful, and he was transformed from a simple, unassuming fellow to a filthy rich CEO of a booming company who flew around on a private jet and found himself the constant center of attention. Shortly thereafter, he began regularly cheating on his wife. A simple life was transformed into a lavish life, and in a lavish life there are casualties—like your family and your God.

So he began to distance himself from his family and his faith. They're inconvenient once you've tasted *more*, and once you've tasted *more* the only thing that can satiate your appetite for *more* is *more*, and so anything or anybody that inconveniently contests your appetite for *more* has to go. So somewhere along the way, a man decided there was probably not a God because he did not want there to be a God. Desire demanded and reason complied. One imagines his logic played out like this: "I like stuff. I want more and more stuff. God contests my desire for more and more stuff. Is there really a God? I mean . . . science, other religions, moral relativity. Probably not. Who cares either way?"

Not everyone who leaves faith has a crisis of faith. Many have a crisis of wanting to do their own thing and not worry about it all too much. 1 Timothy 6:9-10 puts it memorably:

> Those who long to be rich, however, stumble into temptation and a trap and many senseless and harmful desires that plunge people into ruin and destruction. For the love of money is the root of all evils. Some people in reaching for it have strayed from the faith. (1 Timothy 6:9-10 NET)

People wander away from the faith not just because they took freshman biology at a state university, or learned about other religions, or discovered that morality can vary from culture to culture, but because they loved money. It could not be said much more plainly, and yet many rigid biblical literalists start reading curiously metaphorically when it comes to money. And though many Christians will seek out accountability when it comes to sexual purity and personal Bible reading, nobody has permission to talk to them about their money. Talking about sex is okay, but money is too intimate. Mammon has done his work.

This personal anecdote of Mammon-induced apostasy leads us to a brief telling of the long, complex, public story by which stuff became the de facto religion of modern culture.

THE GOODS LIFE

Antoine de Saint-Exupéry has some fantastic advice on how to build a ship: "If you want to build a ship, don't drum up people to collect wood and don't assign them tasks and work, but rather teach them to long for the endless immensity of the sea."

Why? Because if you want people to do something (in this case, build a boat), you must first teach them to love and desire something (the immensity of the sea). So what do you love and desire, and why do you love and desire it?

It's probably hard to explain. Of course you know what you *should* love and desire, but those were not the questions. What *do* you love and desire, and *why* do you love and desire it? If you're like me, you struggle to answer clearly because what you desire isn't a list of specific things but a vision of a certain kind of life.

I want that aforementioned jet ski because I instinctively associate it with a larger vision of a flourishing life where I am happy, whole, successful, and important. And I want that life. I want nothing more than that life. And I want that life so badly because it has captured my imagination. It hasn't grabbed me by the brain but by the guts. Deep beneath all my thinking and reasoning, I am motivated by a gut-level vision of the true, good, and beautiful that I have imbibed through a lifelong process of conditioning, and in that vision, I see me riding a jet ski.

And what is true of my jet ski and me is more or less true of you and most of Western culture at large at this particular moment in time. Mammon has made the endless acquisition and disposal of stuff the operative religion of the "modern" world and has done so by capturing our imagination with a vision of the good life as the goods life. To make a long story somewhat short, a few foundational societal forces were set in motion a few hundred years ago, and these forces made stuff the new religion.

Religion has always killed people; of course, secularism has too. Religion has killed its millions, secularism its ten millions, in just the past hundred years. These deaths are terrible and tragic and became particularly troubling during the Reformation, wherein relentless theological controversies led to the split between Catholics and Protestants and years of nations warring against nations and people killing people in the name of religion. How do you stop people from killing each other in the name of religion? Sequester religion and place it firmly within the sphere of the private and personal so that people are free to believe whatever they want within the walls of their own lives yet not free to leverage political power and violence for religion's sake.

This is the basic rationale behind the modern split between church and state, and the rationale is salient. I am of the opinion that any "god" who asks you to kill in his or her name is not a "god" worth your time. But it did leave culture with a certain vacuum because religion, like it or not, has always been the glue holding cultures together. We are truly *homo religiosus*. And so where do we turn when we've lost the religious ties that bind us together? This was Mammon's chance, so he took us to a very high mountain, showed us all the kingdoms of the world, and said, "All of this I will give to you if you'll just get busy making, buying, and throwing away lots and lots of stuff" (see Matthew 4:8-9).

And make, buy, and throw away stuff we did, on an unprecedented scale, and we discovered how very much we liked it. After all, why get so worked up about religion when you can go shopping instead? Why die for a deity when you can amuse yourself to death with toys? Welcome to the age of "amoral consumerama," where to be is to buy and it is our buying that holds us together. "Amid the hyperpluralism of divergent truth claims, metaphysical beliefs, moral values, and life priorities, ubiquitous practices of consumerism are more than anything else the cultural glue that holds Western societies together. . . . Whatever our differences, acquisitiveness unites us."

In other words, so long as we're busy creating, consuming, and trashing stuff, we won't think too hard about our differences. On a related note, this is why the history of capitalism and secularism are basically the same tale told from different angles: "secularization is simply developed capitalism in its . . . cultural manifestation." Our desire for the unfettered freedom to take and throw away means we must do away with any authority (religious, cultural, social) that might attempt to restrain us. Many devout Christians mourn the modern collapse of traditional values and morality, all the while vociferously advocating the very unfettered consumerama that inevitably devours all values and morality. The institution of marriage is certainly under attack, and Mammon is the primary culprit, because if you've been conditioned to endlessly take and throw away in every other area of your life, why would marriage be any different?

Of course, no group of sinister politicians met together with Mammon in the dark corner of a smoke-filled room to rationally hammer all this out. Again, Mammon did not offer arguments for why stuff would make us happy; Mammon just gave us stuff and trusted our hearts to do the rest. And it's amazing what humans are capable of once we set our hearts to it. We have so much stuff. We have unleashed breathtaking technology so we can more efficiently make, buy, and throw away ever more stuff. To be fair, some of this is good and has enormously alleviated poverty in some parts of the world. Though also to be fair, it has created unimaginable poverty in other parts of the world, but we've spared ourselves the pain of having to see the horrendous conditions of those who make our stuff ("Don't ask, don't tell; just consume"). We're not barbarians. We just think

Jesus is wrong, and we can serve God and Mammon so long as we set our mind to it.

This is a bleak picture, but perhaps some bleak strokes are needed to arouse us from our stuff-induced coma. And this brings us back to my dead-serious and only mildly ridiculous suggestion that far more people are losing faith because of stuff than because of science.

THERE ARE NO ATHEISTS IN A SLUM

I've been told there are no atheists in a foxhole. I suspect this is somewhat true, but I have another hyperbolic apologetic observation: there are no atheists in a slum. Or less hyperbolically: there are far fewer atheists in a slum than in a penthouse. Admittedly, that's an impression, but I do think some numbers back it up.

For example, in America, most self-described atheists are young, white, educated males. Good luck finding research on the economic status of atheists, but I feel safe venturing that many (most?) white, educated, male Americans are affluent. So here's another impression: atheism seems a rather privileged position to take. Personally, my moments of atheistic temptation often come sitting in a lush, leather chair in a trendy coffee shop, sipping on a five-dollar cup of imported coffee, doing my Kierkegaard impersonation, philosophizing about humanity's deep melancholy. If I don't think about it, who will? It's tough having to sit in leather chairs, sip on imported coffee, and think about the wretchedness and squalor so many endure. A lesser man might not be up to it. What would the proletarian masses do without me thinking about all this for them?

Karl Marx famously declared that religion is the opiate of the masses—a crutch the ignorant lean on to cope with life. In fuller context, here is what he said: "Religion is the sigh of the oppressed creature, the heart of a heartless world, and the soul of soulless conditions. It is the opium of the people." I don't think there is any debating this is true—religion does comfort the masses. So I have no qualms with Marx's initial observation, although I would change the final sentence. Marx says religion is the opium of the masses, but it would be truer to say religion is the hope of the poor. Marx thought that hope was an illusion, but Marx wasn't poor.

The poor are more religious than the rich. Why? Because the poor are ignorant or because the rich have mammon on their breath? Has Prometheus really been unbound or is he just Mammon's puppet? I would wager the latter. Religion is the hope of the poor. Stuff is the opiate of the privileged.

We should not romanticize abject poverty. It is a plague. And yet when I am in a slum, I am never much tempted by atheism. I acutely feel the weight of evil and suffering. My heart is shattered. I do not feel happy I believe in God. I feel terrible and torn and conflicted, but when I am in a slum, I do believe in God. I *want* to believe in God. A primal desire for God wells up within me. Because I cannot *not* want there to be a God who enters the slums to gather the bloodied and forgotten—a God who washes their feet and places a crown on their brow.

So if and when we find ourselves sitting in a comfy chair, writhing in existential, contemplative angst over science and other religions and moral relativity, reading a book (like this one!), pondering apostasy because it's all too much to bear, I have a suggestion that was given to me by another. Sell all you possess, give the money to the poor, pursue a life of simple faithfulness in imitation of Christ, and see what happens (Luke 18:18-27). Jesus says this will happen:

> Do not store up for yourselves treasures on earth, where moth
> and rust destroy, and where thieves break in and steal. But

store up for yourselves treasures in heaven, where neither moth nor rust destroys, and where thieves do not break in or steal; for where your treasure is, there your heart will be also. (Matthew 6:19-21)

This text is often used to teach us that where and how we spend our money reveals what we truly love. And while that is true, it is not Jesus' point. Jesus' point is not that the location of our "treasure" reveals the state of our heart, but that the state of our heart is determined by the location of our treasure. Jesus' point is this: if you want to love the true, good, and beautiful, then give away your stuff to the true, good, and beautiful. Your habits condition your heart to love certain things. If you have habits of making stuff your treasure, then your heart will grow to love stuff (and not love, or much believe in, anything or anybody that challenges your love of stuff—like God). If you have habits of making the bloodied and forgotten your treasure (as Christ did), then your heart will grow to love the bloodied and forgotten (and the God who loves them too).

Sound crazy? Well, what do you have to lose? Your stuff? Do you want stuff or a soul? You might just have to choose. You cannot serve God and mammon.

*H*ell is difficult to talk about. It is difficult to talk about because Scripture does not talk about it much or in much detail, and when this is the case, inquiring minds fill in the blanks for themselves. Some find blasphemous the belief that hell is eternal, conscious torment, and some find blasphemous the rejection of a hell that is eternal, conscious torment. In these cases, it is helpful to open some imaginative space to faithfully explore what the nexus of what Scripture, theology, and reason teach on the matter. What follows is that—not a systematic treatise on hell, but a recollection of a conversation I once had regarding what would happen if Hitler got five minutes in heaven, and what that might tell us about hell.

"I BELIEVE IN HELL, BUT I'M NOT HAPPY ABOUT IT"

"I believe in hell, but I'm not happy about it."

These were the first words out of her mouth. Weeks earlier she had asked to come speak with me, which was unusual because she was an elderly lady who was very independent and did not make a habit of scheduling pastoral visits. I wondered what was on her mind and, it turns out, it was hell.

And while I'm sure there was a personal story behind her questions (there always is), I did not pry because she did not offer, and instead I opted to take up her questions as she presented them: biblically, theologically, rationally. She started by laying her cards on the table: she believed in hell but wasn't happy about it. Why? She believed in hell because she felt the Bible taught it, the church had historically confirmed it, and that, depending on her mood, it made a good deal of sense that people like Hitler would experience eternity there.

But she was not happy about it because, well, "eternal conscious torment." I mean, have you ever really thought about what you're claiming to believe in when you claim to believe in eternal conscious torment? How is it possible that God could go from unconditionally welcoming even the vilest sinners to, immediately upon death, torturing them *forever* and, according to some, rather enjoying it? Some take a certain perverse delight in having the intestinal fortitude to affirm eternal conscious torment without flinching, but, so far as she could tell, there was no virtue in being a moral cretin. So, she confessed, she'd been moved to revisit her thoughts on hell, even though she'd held them her entire life. Are Christians really supposed to believe Jesus Christ will torture all unrepentant sinners for eternity?

For the sake of disclosure, I believe in hell but am not happy about it either. I think it's terrible to be happy about it. When I shared this with her, her eyes lit up, she looked around, leaned forward, and then whispered, "You know, there are those verses that seem to teach some sort of universal reconciliation." Indeed there are.

Romans 5:18: "So then as through one transgression there resulted condemnation to all men, even so through one act of righteousness there resulted justification of life to all men."

Romans 11:32: "For God has shut up all in disobedience so that He may show mercy to all."

1 John 2:2: He Himself [Jesus] is the propitiation for our sins; and not for ours only, but also for *those of* the whole world.

John 12:32: "And I, if I am lifted up from the earth, will draw all men to Myself."

Colossians 1:15-20: "He is the image of the invisible God, the firstborn of all creation. For by Him all things were created, *both* in the heavens and on earth, visible and invisible, whether thrones or dominions or rulers or authorities—all things have been created through Him and for Him. He is before all things, and in Him all things hold together. He is also head of the body, the church; and He is the beginning, the firstborn from the dead, so that He Himself will come to have first place in everything. For it was the *Father's* good pleasure for all the fullness to dwell in Him, and through Him to reconcile all things to Himself."

What have we learned? That Jesus has justified all people, atoned for the sins of all people, reconciled all people, and will draw all people to himself. Commenting specifically on John 12:32, New Testament scholar Frederick Dale Bruner says it lucidly: "The whole human race has been reconciled to God."

And while we could cite more texts, Colossians 1:15-20 is all you need to establish that the Bible clearly teaches universal reconciliation. One need only pay attention to the word *all*. When we're told Christ is the firstborn of all creation, does *all* literally mean *all*? Yes. When we're told all things were created through Him and for Him, does *all* literally mean *all*? Yes. When we're told He is before all things and holds all things together, does *all* literally mean *all*? Yes. When we're told all the fullness of deity dwells in Him, does *all* literally mean *all*? Yes.

So how is it possible that when we're told God has reconciled all things to Himself through Christ, *all* doesn't literally mean *all*? I don't think it is possible. I think we must acknowledge that Colossians 1 explicitly teaches the reconciliation of all things to God, through Jesus. That established, the real question (as it always is) is not so much what Scripture says but what it means, and this is where things get tricky.

HITLER, HEAVEN, FIVE MINUTES

The Bible teaches hell. I do not know many people who seriously dispute this, but what the Bible's teaching on hell means is the subject of much debate. Could it be a bluff of sorts, goading people toward repentance? Sounds like evangelism by psychological terrorism to me. Could it be real but not eternal? Basically like purgatory? A place to undergo the fires of sanctification on the road to glory? The Protestant in me gets a bit uncomfortable here, but C. S. Lewis did play around with something like this in *The Great Divorce*. Or could it be real but not eternal in the sense that it is more like the ontological death penalty than unending torture? You won't be tortured forever; you'll just cease to exist—"Fear Him who is able to destroy both soul and body in hell" (Matthew 10:28). Annihilation? I am barely scratching the surface, but suffice it to say, debates abound, which brings us to Hitler and his five minutes in heaven.

The Bible teaches universal reconciliation. The Bible teaches hell. How do we reconcile universal reconciliation and hell? Well, if Hitler got five minutes in heaven, do you think he would like it?

He cautiously approaches the pearly gates. He's suspicious about the whole venture—why has God granted him clemency? What's in it for God? Nobody fools the Führer! He'll get to the bottom of it, and probably come away with a kingdom in tow. A few paces out, the gates open and light pours forth, hurting his dim eyes. He shields them, and, lo and behold, here comes Saint Peter to greet him—Saint

Peter the Jew! Hitler is not amused. He blows past Peter and makes his way inside, where he quickly spies a group of angels. He strides over to them and dispenses marching orders. He'll have a new Reich assembled in no time. But the smallest angel smiles, puts his arm over Hitler's shoulder, and says, "Oh, dear little Adolf—that's not how things work around here. But you'll get the hang of it soon enough."

Dear little Adolf!? Those angels will regret their patronizing kindness. Onward!

Finally, he reaches the center of heaven, where all of creation worships a little, bitty, broken lamb (Revelation 5). "Pathetic," thinks Hitler. Then the broken lamb, Jesus the Messiah, King of the universe, spots Hitler and runs over to him, hugs him, and says, "Adolf, I forgive you and have a place for you."

Hitler's response is visceral: "Get your weak little hands off me! This is ridiculous. I don't want your love. I don't need your forgiveness. Do you know who I am? I am a big deal. I conquered lots of Europe for a few years back in the day. I don't bow down before people; people bow down before me." Better to reign in hell than serve in heaven, said Milton, and Hitler agrees.

If Hitler got five minutes in heaven, it would probably feel like an eternity in hell.

With this scene in mind, let's consider a few thoughts.

THE PARABLE OF THE ONION

I know people who do not like to be loved. I know people who despise forgiveness. I know people who hate mercy. And I know that sounds crazy, but I know that you know people like that too, and perhaps you have been someone like that. The heart is resilient but remarkably impressionable, and if we make habits of hatred, wickedness, and cruelty, we will become people who love hatred, wickedness, and cruelty and hate love, forgiveness, and mercy. We are all always in the process of becoming someone we just might have to be forever: "What if death only forever fixes us as the kind of person we are at death?" What if eternity is simply the process by which "everything becomes more and more itself"?

These are sobering thoughts, but they make sense. Take Dostoyevsky's fantastical parable of the onion. A very wicked woman dies and is tossed into the lake of fire. Her guardian angel devises a plan to rescue her. Because she was so wicked, the angel does not have much to work with—nothing, in fact, except for an onion the woman once pulled out of her garden and gave to a beggar. The angel asks God if this good deed might be enough to get her out of hell, and God has a mediating proposal: "You take that onion . . . hold it out to her in the lake, and let her take hold of it and be pulled out. And if you can pull her out of the lake, let her come to Paradise, but if the onion breaks, then the woman must stay where she is."

It's a deal!

So the angel stands on the shore of the lake of fire, holds out the onion, and tells her to catch hold so she can be pulled out. She does and is almost free when everyone else in the lake sees what is happening and grabs hold of her feet so they can be pulled out with her. Because she is a very wicked woman, she begins thrashing about, kicking them off, yelling, "I'm to be pulled out, not you. It's my onion, not yours." And as soon as she says this, the onion breaks in half and she falls back into the lake of fire, where she remains to this day.

Take care of who you're becoming. You might have to live with yourself forever.

CONSUMING FIRE

God is a consuming fire (Hebrews 12:29). In speaking of new creation, some theologians liken it to Moses' burning bush in Exodus 3, on fire but not consumed. God is the consuming fire that does and doesn't consume. Perhaps we could understand it like this.

When we die, we are wholly reconciled to that fire whose sparks we are, and that reconciliation will be experienced in very different ways. For some, the blazing fire of God's love will be experienced as bliss, but for others it will be experienced as wrath. For some it will be heaven, but for others it will be hell. As Hart says, "What we call hell is nothing but the rage and remorse of the soul that will not yield itself to love. . . . The wrathful soul experiences the transfiguring and deifying fire of love not as bliss but as chastisement and despair."

Like frigid hands plunged into a bowl of hot water, the immersion into God's new world will be an unpleasant baptism for those with icy hearts. Again, this is not hard to believe, and we see it even now.

So how do we reconcile universal reconciliation and hell? Maybe like this: God will love everyone forever, but some will hate him for it. Hell is merely the fire of love experienced as the lake of fire by frostbitten souls. Hell is "the suffering of being unable to love." When we live against the grain of the universe, we are filleted by icy splinters and even heaven becomes hell: "There will never be beings unloved by God. . . . Hell, as refusal of divine love, always exists on one side only: on the side of him who persists in creating it for himself."

So far as God is concerned, the pearly gates will always be open (Revelation 21:25), but human rebellion is nothing if not a stubborn mystery, and I have no problem believing some would rather reign in hell than serve in heaven. Tim Keller agrees: "If you think hell is a place where people are crawling up the sides saying, 'Let me out, let me out, God.' And God is up there at the top saying, 'No, it's too late. You had your chance. Haha!' and shuts the lid on them, then you really don't understand human nature or what the Bible is saying about hell." Or in C. S. Lewis's striking phrase, "the doors of hell are locked on the *inside*."

OF OXEN AND ASSES

"Yes, yes—I've thought similar things," she said, and leaned in even closer. Then, after looking around once more, again she whispered: "But do you think that, given eternity, God might be able to straighten and warm those crooked, frozen hearts and coax them out of their homemade dungeon?"

I smiled because her question brought to mind one of my favorite quotes, spoken hundreds of years ago by a Pietist named Christian Gottlieb Barth: "Anyone who does not believe in the universal restoration is an ox, but anyone who teaches it is an ass." Though I admire his candor, Barth goes too far, so I like to amend his quotation: anyone who does not *hope* for universal restoration is an ox, but anyone who teaches it is an ass.

She chuckled and asked me to explain further.

Based on the teaching of Scripture, it's clear to me that hell is real and that there is the distinct possibility and likelihood it will be inhabited. But God owes me no definitive explanations on such things, so just as God desires that all would be saved (1 Timothy 2:4), so I hope that all will be saved. What kind of Christian wouldn't? And yet God gives me no permission to *believe* all will be saved, much less bank on it, so I spend my time fulfilling the Great Commission instead of proselytizing people into universalism. As C. S. Lewis asserts, "It may be . . . that all will be well, and all manner of things will be well. But it's ill talking of such questions."

I think God looks for excuses to let people in, not keep people out, and that is my only opinion in regards to all the worthless speculation about who will be "in" and who will be "out." I think God wants a full house: "I am thoroughly convinced that God will let everyone into heaven who, in his considered opinion, can stand it." But I also think the "fires in heaven may be hotter than those in the other place," and many won't be able to stand the heat.

All this brings me to something else: heaven and hell will be filled with surprises. I'm thinking especially of the parable of the sheep and goats in Matthew 25. If the stakes weren't so high, the whole scene would be hilarious. The sheep are welcomed into eternal life and the goats eternal punishment, and none of them sees it coming. The goats are particularly confused: "Where were you? When did we see you? We're being judged for *that*!? Cups of water not passed out? Prison visits not made?"

Sometimes I fancy that upon arriving in heaven, all of us will be confronted with our worst enemy and will assume, naturally, that we're in hell. Then Jesus will show up, smile, invite us to sit at a table together, and lead us in an improvised riff on Psalm 23: "You prepare a table for me in the presence of my enemies, and then invite my enemies, and sit them beside me, because it's their table too." Welcome to the kingdom of God!

Legend has it someone once asked Karl Barth if she would see her loved ones again in heaven, to which Barth responded, "Not just those you loved!" Yes—you will see loved ones, and unloved ones, and enemies in the kingdom of God. Surprises will abound. Speaking of Revelation 21 and 22, N. T. Wright reminds us to make room for the surprises of God's new world: "There is a great mystery here. . . . This is not at all to cast doubt on the reality of final judgment. . . . It is to say that God is always the God of surprises." Similarly, the great missiologist Lesslie Newbigin has pleaded that we "stop arguing about whether or not people are going to be saved. I don't believe that is

our business. . . . We know from the teaching of Jesus that one thing
is sure—that at the end of time there will be surprises." Or as Hans
Urs von Balthasar has suggested, instead of declaring who is in and
who is out, we are required only "not to let go of love."

And whatever else heaven and hell will be, they will be places
where mercy triumphs over judgment (James 2:13).

OXYGEN

"Well you've talked me out of being a universalist."

She was smiling and sitting back more comfortably in her seat
now, and this time, I chuckled. "But," she said, "what do you think
happens to all those ruined souls that have barricaded themselves
into hell?"

I had another meeting in a few minutes, so I considered adjourning,
but I had been kicking this question around for some time, so I ap-
preciated the opportunity translate my mental ramblings into words.
"Maybe something like this . . ."

Deep in the belly of every human burns the fire that is the image
of God. I do not think that image can be lost in life, though many
seem hell-bent on disfiguring it beyond recognition. But that flame
is something we have on loan, and a flame needs oxygen to survive.
And hell is a place without oxygen, a place of utter self-absorption,
a place where people cave in completely upon themselves.

Think of the parable of the rich man and Lazarus in Luke 16:19-31.
There is a rich man who lives in splendor and a poor man named
Lazarus who lives covered in sores and begging for scraps from the
rich man's table. As humans are prone to do, they die, and—surprise!—
Lazarus awakens in heaven and the rich man in Hades. And the first
thing the rich man does upon rousing is ask Father Abraham to send

Lazarus over with some water: "I'm parched! Send over that beggar. What's his name? Lazarus—yes, send Lazarus over."

Even in life after death, he treats Lazarus like a peon. Even in life after death, he thinks Lazarus is his servant. There is no repentance, regret, remorse, or relenting. Everything that was just becomes more and more itself. I have a hunch that rich man is still in Hades, ringing his little bell, waiting for Lazarus to come serve him that cup of water.

But perhaps the ringing of that little bell will eventually stop. Perhaps the rich man's self-absorption will absorb him. Due to the lack of oxygen that is lack of love, the flame of the divine will go out—ontological suicide by self-inflicted smothering. Wright hints at something similar:

> It seems to me . . . that if it is possible . . . for human beings to choose to live more and more out of tune with the divine intention, to reflect the image of God less and less, there is nothing to stop them finally ceasing to bear that image, and so to be, as it were, beings who were once human but are not now. Those who persistently refuse to follow Jesus . . . will by their own choice become less and less like him, that is, less and less truly human. . . .
>
> I see nothing in the New Testament to make me reject the possibility that some, perhaps many, of God's human creatures do choose, and will choose, to dehumanize themselves completely. Nor do I see anything to make me suppose that God, who gave his human creatures the risky gift of freedom and choice, will not honour that choice. . . . This, I think, is the way in which something like the traditional doctrine of hell can be restated in the present day.

"So hell as a sort of self-annihilation?" she asked.

"That's my working theory," I answered.

"Well," she said, "I've heard worse explanations." I smiled and said that so long as my explanation wasn't the worst she'd heard, I felt like my work was done.

She gathered up her belongings, walked to the threshold of the door, and with a modest grin said, "I still believe in hell, and I'm still not happy about it."

CHAPTER ELEVEN

FAITH, DOUBT, AND LOVE

THE REAL REMEDY

*W*hat happens when you've been faithful with your doubts—told God the truth about them, ruthlessly interrogated them, run yourself into the ground laboring for answers to appease them, relentlessly defaced them with defiant graffiti—and you still can't shake your vertigo-induced skepticism? Maybe it's the evil or the silence or the science or the stuff or some combination thereof or something else altogether, but the doubts will not go away, the terminal skepticism is spreading, all attempts to throw your six ant arms and legs up in equal portions terror, bliss, and surrender have failed miserably, and you're such a mess you begin to wonder if Judas's betraying blood runs through your veins. It happens. It has happened to me. What do we do then?

It's a question that evokes another moment from Dostoyevsky's *The Brothers Karamazov*. A mother has traveled to see a wise and revered priest. Days earlier the priest had prayed for her little girl, and the girl had experienced healing, so she's come back to thank him. She does so but is immediately overwhelmed by anguish and the need to ask the priest something. Despite her momentary joy, a deep sadness weighs on her shoulders because she bears a terminal case of skepticism. So she cries out to the priest:

> Let me say what I could not say last time, what I dared not say. I have been suffering for so long! I am suffering! Forgive me!

I am suffering! . . . I suffer . . . from lack of faith. . . . Life after
death—it is such an enigma! And no one, no one can solve
it. . . . And I say to myself: "What if I've been believing all my
life, and when I come to die there's nothing but weeds growing
on my grave?" . . . How—how can I get my faith back? I only
believed when I was a little child, mechanically, without thinking
of anything. How, how is one to prove it? . . . How can I convince myself?

Her words have the tonal depth that marks the truth. She's at the
end of her rope—no stones left unturned, no bullets left in the chamber.
What does she do, what do we do, when all else has failed and our
faith is still failing us?

In 1 Corinthians, Paul is writing to the church at Corinth, and it's
clear that he and they have very different understandings of what it
means to be people filled with the Spirit. Indeed, the Corinthians are
very spiritual people—they have all this knowledge, all these spiritual
gifts, and all this faith. And they think their knowledge, gifts, and
faith are the epitome of spiritual maturity. But Paul has other ideas,
and in 1 Corinthians 13, he lays them out.

In 1 Corinthians 13:2, Paul says, "If I have all faith, so as to remove
mountains, but do not have love, I am nothing." Here Paul is channeling Matthew 17:20, where Jesus tells us we can move mountains
around if we have faith the size of a mustard seed, and Paul's point
is harsh. Perhaps you have "all faith"; perhaps you walk around with
an unshakeable confidence in the promises of God; perhaps your
faith is constantly altering the earth's topography because it's constantly
rearranging the mountains—that might well be so, and you might
well be nothing. Because it's possible to have all the faith in the world
and still be nothing.

Then in 1 Corinthians 13:11-13, Paul pushes his point to its consummation:

> When I was a child, I talked like a child, I thought like a child, I reasoned like a child. When I became a man, I put the ways of childhood behind me. For now we see only a reflection as in a mirror; then we shall see face to face. Now I know in part; then I shall know fully, even as I am fully known.
>
> And now these three remain: faith, hope, and love. But the greatest of these is love. (1 Corinthians 13:11-13 NIV)

Paul makes an analogy that effectively calls the Corinthians' knowledge, gifts, and faith childish and immature. Why? Because they aren't eternal; they will not last. For now they are important and helpful, but they will be done away with one day. They will not have a place in God's new world. They are child's play. Then comes Paul's famous triad of faith, hope, and love, which he uses throughout his letters to describe the essence of Christian living.

Faith, hope, and love—everything God wants for us is reducible to these three things. Then comes the shockingly overlooked phrase, "But the greatest of these is love."

We cannot live well without faith, hope, or love. But love, says Paul, is even greater than faith and hope. Faith and hope will be done away with one day, but love is forever, grounded in the very being of God. We are never more like God than when we love and are loved. So could it be that the ultimate remedy for our doubt is not faith, but love?

I DO BELIEVE AND I DON'T BELIEVE

Mark 9:14-27 tells the story of a little boy and his father.

Jesus comes down from some time on the mountain and steps into a scene of chaos. There's a huge crowd, there's shouting, and at the center of it all there's the little boy and his father. The boy is very sick—demon possessed, in fact, as he has been for a long time. When a fit hits him, he collapses, foams at the mouth, and stiffens out like a board. He has thrown himself into fires and lakes. And perhaps the only person more broken than this little boy is his father. Can you imagine it? Watching your child in agony, unable to fix him? Unable to make it better? Unable to protect him? Some of you can imagine it because you have lived it. So this broken father brings his broken boy to Jesus, desperately hoping something can be done.

"If you can do anything, then please take pity on us and help!" cries the father to Jesus, and this rubs Jesus the wrong way. "*If* I can do anything? Do you know who you're talking to? All things are possible if you believe, so do you believe, father?" It's the first time in the Gospel of Mark Jesus has made faith a precondition for healing. What follows is one of the most unashamedly human moments in all of Scripture. The father cries out, "I do believe; help my unbelief" (Mark 9:24).

This father believes, but he also doubts. He's a man of faith and a man of doubt. He's torn, conflicted, walking the tightrope. "I do believe, but I don't believe too"—that's what he says to Jesus, and if you've got a heart beating inside your chest then you know exactly what he means because you do believe but you don't believe too.

So Jesus pauses to look around—at the father, at his boy, at the gathering crowd—and then says, "Demon, get out of that little boy and never come near him again." The boy crumbles, cries out, convulses, and then becomes deathly still. And Jesus takes him by the hand and raises him up—healed, free, redeemed.

And it was not perfect, doubtless faith that healed this little boy—it was love.

By all accounts, it seems he was healed because his father loved him. He was healed because his father was willing to make a scene, to make a fool of himself, to do whatever it took to help his son. He did not have the faith to move mountains, but he had the love to take his pickaxe and chop down a mountain stone by stone. What this father lacked in faith he made up for in love. And now these three remain: faith, hope, and love. But the greatest of these is love.

THE GREATEST OF THESE IS (NOT) FAITH

We forgot this truth somewhere along the way. Ask the average Christian what God wants most from us and a healthy percentage (perhaps a majority, certainly of Protestants) will say faith. What's most important is that you have faith. The greatest of these is faith. It was not always this way, and the elevation of faith to the status of supreme theological virtue is perhaps best understood as an unintended consequence of the Reformation.

As Brad Gregory describes it, the Reformation's fierce theological disputes had the effect of "placing unprecedented emphasis on interior assent to the propositional content of doctrinal truth claims. . . . It risked making Christianity seem more a matter of what one believed than of how one lived—of making the faith a . . . matter of one's soul and mind, *rather than* a matter of what one does with one's body." Faith, understood as believing in truths about God, became the be all and end all of Christian living: "Promoted from its traditional subordination to *caritas* [love] among the three theological virtues [faith, hope, and love], faith was redefined by Lutheran and Reformed Protestant theologians as the all-or-nothing cornerstone of Christian life, the result of no human merit, goodness, effort, or cooperation with God."

In other words, endless theological fights and a proper desire to maintain the supremacy of divine grace over human effort caused faith to leapfrog love as the cardinal Christian virtue. Faith became an end in itself. The greatest of these became faith instead of love.

But faith is not an end in itself. Faith is not a destination. Faith is not "believing in truths about God." Faith is a divinely gifted disposition of the heart that helps us faithfully arrive at the destination: namely, love. Faith is a means to love. Faith, as von Balthasar says, is "ordered primarily to the inconceivability of God's love":

> Love alone is credible; nothing else can be believed, and nothing else ought to be believed. This is the achievement, the "work" of faith . . . to believe that there is such a thing as love, absolute love, and that there is nothing higher or greater than it.

When asked what was the greatest commandment, Jesus did not say it was to have faith so as to move mountains without the slightest shred of doubt. No, Jesus said the greatest commandment was to love God and love neighbor. The virtue of faith is that it trains us to love and be loved. It is a posture of trusting surrender to the love of God. It is necessary because love requires vulnerability, and vulnerability requires surrender, and surrender requires trust. As Alexander Schmemann writes, "Faith itself is the acceptance not of this or that 'proposition' about Christ, but of Christ Himself as the Life and the light of life. . . . [Faith's] starting point is not 'belief' but love."

I suspect many of us cannot shake our doubts because we are striving for faith instead of love. And while the relationship between faith and love is close and complex, this much is clear: the simplistic formulation in which faith and love relate in a strictly linear fashion wherein faith produces love is wholly inadequate. Faith can produce love, but love can also produce faith. Many have so emphasized faith's ability to create love that they have forgotten love's ability to create faith.

To return to an idea mentioned in chapter nine, we have vastly overestimated our ability to *think* ourselves through the world. We think we can think our way into proper actions and beliefs. We think we can think our way into faith. Sit around thinking about that all you want, but the results are in: it doesn't work. Sitting around and thinking about faith conditions you to be a person who sits around and thinks about faith. But when Jesus asks us to follow him, he is not asking us to sit around and think about faith. He is asking us to get up and do things with our hands and feet. A thick instead of thin faith does not precede following Jesus; it follows following. So if you'd like more faith, quit trying to think your way into faith and instead, empowered by the grace of God, go love your way into faith.

And this brings us back to that mother with the healed daughter and terminal case of skepticism, standing before the wise, old priest, pouring her skeptical heart out: "I suffer from lack of faith. How can I get my faith back? How can I convince myself? I can't stand it! It's deadly!" To this the priest responds,

> No doubt. But there's no proving it, though you can be convinced of it . . . by the experience of active love. Strive to love your neighbor actively and constantly. In so far as you advance in love you will grow surer of the reality of God and of the immortality of the soul. If you attain perfect self-forgetfulness in the love of your neighbor, then you will believe without doubt. Doubt will no longer be able to enter your soul. This has been tried. This is certain.

Dostoyevsky's priest seems to be channeling 1 John 3:18-19: "Little children, let us not love with word or with tongue, but in deed and truth. We will know by this that we are of the truth, and will assure our heart before Him."

The ultimate remedy for doubt is neither perfect, doubtless faith nor being honest about not having much faith. The ultimate remedy for doubt is love because love creates faith. Whatever faith you have, you have because you're loved—God loves you and that's why you have faith. We experience God's love and it creates faith, then we share God's love and it creates faith too! When we love in deed and truth, our hearts find assurance (1 John 3:18-19). Love is the way to assurance. I know this from experience.

FAITH, DOUBT, AND LOVE

A year had passed since the earthquake that shook the top of the world. In light of the horrendous suffering it caused, it felt trite to think about it as the earthquake that rattled my faith, but I couldn't help myself. The brute juxtaposition of the world's beauty and the terror it displayed had opened a fault line deep in my heart. I could not un-see what I had seen, could not un-feel what I had felt. For a variety of reasons—some of which I understand but many of which I do not and may never—I was not the same after the earthquake. I will never be the same.

As I packed my bags for my return trip to Nepal, I began to feel ill. Hoping it was nothing, I kept packing, but as evening fell I spiked a high fever. What followed was one of the most miserable nights of my life.

I lay in bed—miserable, sweating profusely, aching all over, running a 103-degree fever—and nasty thoughts started running through my head. In the past forty-eight hours, two planes had gone down in Nepal. (Due to the altitude, mountainous terrain, severe weather, and inexperienced pilots, Nepal is the most dangerous place in the world to fly.) My faith was fragile; I'd feared I would lose it at numerous points over the past year. I did not want to leave my wife and son. I did not feel like traveling to the other side of the world in service of a faith I had lost much faith in. And then the voice of my inner atheist (we've all got one) started rattling off every deep and dark doubt that lurks down in my soul.

"Let's level with each other, Austin. We both know that you don't really *know* if any of this Christianity stuff is real. I won't argue probability percentages with you, but what do you think the chances really are? Sixty/forty? You want to fly across the world for a wager like that? And not to be emotionally manipulative, but how many children have to die before you sober up and see that life is a cold, ugly tragedy? What must happen for you to accept the obvious fact that the universe could not care less what happens to anybody? And while we're at it, what kind of father leaves his family to fly across the world in the name of a faith he is not and could not possibly be certain of?"

With both my physical and theological immune systems down, I could not put up much of a fight. I was tired of fighting. And I wish I could tell you that at the end of this dark night of the soul, the voice of God came to the rescue, banishing my doubts and filling me with peace and assurance. Faith did not come to my rescue that night. I got up early the next morning and boarded my flight, but faith didn't get me on that plane—love did.

And let me be clear—I don't mean some sort of abstract, fluffy, saccharine sentimentalism. I mean I lay there in bed, sweating, miserable, filled with doubt, and yet I thought about the pastors over in Nepal I was going to serve and train—men and women who courageously labor under harsh conditions, who are often outcasts in their villages, who have so little training from which to draw. And while I could doubt almost every single article of faith I had ever held dear,

I simply could not doubt that going there and serving them would be an act of love. I could not doubt that if I tried, and I most certainly did. And while over there, a miracle of sorts occurred.

My doubts did not magically disappear, but they gradually became less and less important, less and less vocal, less and less oppressive. And my faith became more and more assured, settled, and resilient. Why?

I would venture it had something to do with the fact that I was so busy loving people, my inner atheist did not have the space or time to set up shop, kick and scream, and pitch his predictable existential fit. Doubt can argue against faith all day long, but doubt stutters and stammers and falls silent before love. Doubt doesn't know how to argue with love. Love tends to make a fool out of doubt. If you don't believe me, then try it.

So when doubt gets down in your bones and skepticism feels terminal, do what you can to make sense of it. Slug it out with the thorny questions, be as skeptical of your skepticism as your skepticism is of everything else, and mine for good answers. But eventually you have to stop sitting around, wishing and hoping and thinking and praying for more faith, get up off your butt, and go love somebody. After all, the greatest person in the eyes of God is not the one with the most faith but the one with the most love. And when all is said and done and we stand before the great white throne, I reckon the question we will be asked is not "Did you doubt?" but "Did you love?"

Faith is not the absence of doubt. Faith is the presence of love.

CHAPTER TWELVE

CHRIST OR THE TRUTH?

A CASE FOR FAITH IN THE WORST CASE

*W*hat happens when you've been faithful with your doubts and tried to nuke them into oblivion with love, but when the smoke clears, some resolute radioactive remnants remain and it appears your faith-filled rebellion is over? Surely there comes a point at which our only choice is to wave the white flag and walk away. What does God expect when he leaves us out in the cold for so long without the faintest warming whisper of love? We're not God, after all. How silent and absent can God be while still expecting us to hang on? There are times it seems God simply asks too much of us. What do we do then?

A small stone sits in an old communion cup in my bedroom. It's a stone I picked up on a Sunday afternoon during a cataclysmically serious and childish moment of mutiny. I had done everything possible to stoke the fires of my faith. I had even done "nothing" and given up. (The Protestant in me always likes to suggest the problem is that I'm trying too hard.) All had failed. Despite my gnawing agnosticism, I had just finished preaching three consecutive services (it's what preachers do), so I had spent most of the morning feeling like a fraud. Sensing it might be time to walk away from it all, I went for a walk.

I ended up at a park near my house where, despite my seditious intentions, I started praying. I told God the truth about what was going on. I told God I didn't think I had it in me to be a pastor anymore. I told God I had never been greedy—asking for burning bushes or parted seas that would put my faith beyond the reach of all doubt—so I struggled to understand why he would not do more or at least something. I told him I was every bit as tired of letting him off the hook as I assumed he was of letting me off the hook. And being self-aware to a fault, I told God I readily conceded he might well be doing a great many things I merely could not sense (because of stubbornness or sin or whatever), but, him being God and all, I was confident he could come up with something to do that I could sense and that would resurrect my faith.

And at about that time, I looked down and saw a small, smooth stone. Without thinking, I found myself kneeling down to pick it up and brooding over how silly it was that I had staked my life on a stone much like this one, only much bigger. I had staked my life on the belief that two thousand years ago a stone rolled away while no one was looking because God had raised Jesus from the dead. "How insane is this!?" I said to myself. "How insane is it that people have lived and died for a belief that, once upon a time, God rolled away a stone to open up a tomb?" And with all the audacity I could muster, I raised that small, smooth stone up into the heavens and in a brazenly explicative-filled rant, told God that if he couldn't be bothered to move this small stone in my hand, I couldn't be bothered to go on believing he had moved a far larger one away from Jesus' grave, once upon a time. It seemed a fair ultimatum to me.

So I stood with that rock thrust into the heavens for about ten minutes. It did not move.

At this point, I would typically start talking myself off the ledge. God has his reasons. God's ways are higher than your ways. God doesn't owe it to you to move rocks on your command. Quit being an ungrateful, petulant brat. All true—if there is a God, of course. But I was tired of stopping at the ledge, and God had forced my hand, so over I went. For the first time in my life, I actually said, "There is no God," and part of me meant it. I put the stone in my pocket, walked back home, and told no one.

The next few days felt like treason. There I was, a pastor who didn't believe in God! Well, I kind of didn't believe in God. Truth be told, I was not capable of not believing in God, so what was really happening is I was actually considering, for the first time, what it would be like to live without God. My treachery only lasted five days, some of which were documented by a few brief journal entries I made on a yellow legal pad. My conclusion: I would rather be wrong about Jesus than right about anything else.

FOOLS

Anyone who says they can definitively prove belief for or against God is a fool. "The fool has said in his heart, 'There is no God'" (Psalm 53:1). And the fool has said in his heart, "There is a God and I can easily prove it. Grab a pen and paper. This won't take long. You'll be on the straight and narrow by sundown." So despite objections from fundamentalist believers and unbelievers, it appears belief in God is an essentially contested belief. We have been arguing about whether or not God exists for thousands of years, and (Lord willing) we will continue to argue about it for thousands more because there is no settling the question once and for all. We can pile up all the evidence on the scales, but the result will not be conclusive enough to make the question go away.

And there is no higher court to which we may appeal. There is no one to adjudicate. There is no missing piece of evidence that will decisively tip the scales. Surely Keith Ward is right when he states that "even with all the empirical evidence at hand, there seems to be no way of establishing one interpretation that will be acceptable to all informed and intelligent people." I know of noted Christians who claim they are Christians because their "high regard for the truth" leaves them no alternative because Christianity is so obviously true, but such an assured assertion is quite obviously false. Then there is noted atheist Richard Dawkins, claiming the "universe that we observe has precisely the properties we should expect if there is, at bottom, no design, no purpose, no evil, no good, nothing but pitiless indifference." And yet here is Richard Dawkins, speaking of design, purpose, evil, and good. Ironies abound. So argue it until you're blue in the face, but the fact that there will always be someone there for you to argue with proves the point. Belief in God is and will probably always be "essentially contested."

As this dawned on me, I was overcome with a conflicted sense of despair and relief—despair because I would never find what I had been looking for (a faith beyond doubt's icy grip), and relief because I could finally stop looking for this something that deep down I had always known I would not find. I was overcome with the sense that I had finally surrendered to the truth.

Unfortunately, the reality of the human situation is that we are forced to act with decisiveness on matters of which we cannot be sure. Belief in God is an essentially contested belief, but this does not let us off the hook. We believe in God, and it makes a difference. We don't believe in God, and it makes a difference. We don't know if, what, or how we believe in God, and it makes a difference. It's cruel and unfair, but it's the truth all the same. So while I had surrendered to an inconvenient yet liberating truth, this did not absolve me of the burden of having to choose whether I would live as if God did, didn't, or maybe did and maybe didn't "exist."

"The fool has said in his heart, 'There is no God.'"

The words of Psalm 53:1 kept coming back to me. What did the psalmist mean? Clearly you don't have to be unintelligent to disbelieve in God. Some of the smartest people on the planet don't believe in God. So is this a mere splash of rhetorical bravado? Is the psalmist hyperbolically overstating his case to intimidate his imaginary pagan interlocutor? How are people fools for refusing to believe in God?

I have referenced nineteenth-century Russian novelist Fyodor Dostoyevsky a few times. To say the least, he was a complex man. Widely considered one of the greatest novelists in recent history, Dostoyevsky was and is praised by a wide range of admirers, from devout believers to militant atheists. He was a man of deep faith but was also capable of shocking wickedness. Although he was not a theologian proper, people are drawn to his novels because of his breathtaking feel for the subtlest and most troubling contours of faith. Simply put, he possessed that rare combination of mental integrity and aesthetic intuition that marks the truest and most beautiful minds. He understands things others struggle to understand because he follows ideas down to their foundations. He clearly expresses concepts others fumble around with because he knows how to frame them. He writes with kinesthetic grace and not just logical precision. And he helped me understand why I would be a fool for not believing in God.

In a private correspondence with a friend, he shared the personal creed that had preserved his faith against the gales of skepticism:

> I want to say to you, about myself, that I am a child of this age, a child of unfaith and scepticism, and probably (indeed I know it) shall remain so to the end of my life. How dreadfully has it tormented me (and torments me even now) this longing for faith, which is all the stronger for the proofs I have against it.

And yet God gives me sometimes moments of perfect peace; in such moments I love and believe that I am loved; in such moments I have formulated my creed, wherein all is clear and holy to me. This creed is extremely simple; here it is: I believe that there is nothing lovelier, deeper, more sympathetic, more rational, more manly, and more perfect than the Saviour; I say to myself with jealous love that not only is there no one else like Him, but that there could be no one. I would even say more: If anyone could prove to me that Christ is outside the truth, and if the truth really did exclude Christ, I should prefer to stay with Christ and not with truth.

CHRIST OR THE TRUTH?

If you had to choose between Christ and the truth, what would you choose?

I understand it's an unthinkable question and a somewhat absurd thought experiment, but try to think about it. If it were proven to you beyond the shadow of a doubt that Christ was not God and that there was no God, would you choose Christ or the truth? Earlier in life, I would have instantly (and naively) sided with the truth, but as I kicked Dostoyevsky's scandalous hypothetical decision around in my mind, I began to sense his meaning.

Once you have glimpsed the beauty of Christ, there really is no going back. It ruins you. The story of the God-man becoming flesh, touching lepers, embracing sinners, drinking wine, preaching a coming kingdom of redemption and revelry, dying for the crimes of every last crook and priest, resurrected as a harbinger of a looming apocalypse of love—once you have heard this story, felt this story, lived this story, everything else will let you down. To truly hear the gospel is to evolve past ever being satisfied with something less. This doesn't mean it's true, but it does mean your moral, imaginative, and existential palate will find all else pathetically bland. Once you've acquired a taste for communion wine, Moscato makes you nauseous. As Alexander Schmemann says:

> Christianity was . . . the end of all natural joy. It revealed its impossibility, its futility, its sadness—because by revealing the perfect man it revealed the abyss of man's alienation from God and the inexhaustible sadness of this alienation. The cross of Christ signified an end of all "natural" rejoicing. . . . From this point of view the sad "seriousness" of modern man is certainly of Christian origin. . . . Since the Gospel was preached in this world, all attempts to go back to a pure "pagan joy," all "renaissances," all "healthy optimisms" were bound to fail.

This is a social fact as much as a personal feeling, and the spasms afflicting the Western world's shift into a post-Christian culture bear this out. "We hold these truths to be self-evident," say the writers of the U.S. Constitution, "that all men are created equal, that they are endowed by their Creator with certain unalienable rights, that among these are life, liberty, and the pursuit of happiness."

One can charitably say this is complete nonsense. There is nothing "self-evident" about the belief that all men are created equal and endowed by their "Creator" with "unalienable rights." It was not self-evident for thousands of years of human history. You do not look around the world and naturally come to the conclusion that all deserve life, liberty, and the pursuit of happiness. It was not reason that endowed all of humanity, prince and pauper alike, with an infinite dignity that is violated at great peril to the transgressor. It was Christ!

Christianity's grip on Western culture has been a mixed bag, but make no mistake, the dawn of Christianity caused a moral eruption that forever changed the way we think about each other. The ideals of equality, justice, and compassion we take for granted as givens are not givens and cannot be taken for granted. Again—"reason" did not give them to us; Christ did.

So while our increasingly secular culture has climbed Jacob's ladder to its lofty ideals, those ideals will plummet back down to earth as the ladder is progressively kicked away. Like a flower plucked from the soil, they will wither. A strictly "secular" society lacks the moral capital to fund ideals like the intrinsic dignity of all human beings, and if it appears it does, this is only because it has smuggled those funds from Christian capital that it still has the luxury of trading on—for now.

I'm not one to mourn the death of Christendom so much as welcome it, but, as Hart suggests, perhaps it is better for a culture to have never loved Christianity than to have loved then lost it:

> When, therefore, Christianity departs, what is left behind? It may be that Christianity is the midwife of nihilism precisely because, in rejecting it, a people necessarily rejects everything except the bare horizon of the undetermined will. No other god can now be found. The story of the crucified God took everything to itself, and so—in departing—takes everything with it. . . .
>
> When the aspiring ape ceases to think himself a fallen angel, perhaps he will inevitably resign himself to being an ape, and then become contented with his lot, and ultimately even rejoice that the universe demands little more from him than an ape's contentment. If nothing else, it seems certain that post-Christian civilization will always lack the spiritual resources, or the organizing myth, necessary to produce anything like the cultural

wonders that sprang up under the sheltering canopy of the religion of the God-man.

In other words, Christianity has "ruined" the world.

Time will tell if the wider Western world can cope with devolving from a society of fallen angels to a cultured jungle of aspiring apes, but if I had to choose between Christ and the truth, I would choose Christ and would be a fool to choose otherwise. How so? Well, I wouldn't be a rational fool so much as I'd be a moral fool. If the truth is "there is no God," then there are no rules—there are only sentiments. Given that there are no rules, what sort of life will I pursue? I've had moments and long seasons of living without Christ, and this is what I've learned: my life is more beautiful with Christ than it is without him.

Don't misunderstand me. I do not mean it is easier; in many senses, it is not. Without Christ I tend to have more money in my bank account, more time for leisure, more nonchalance toward the beggar rummaging through the dumpster as I wait in line at Starbucks. I mean that imitation of Christ creates in me a moral imagination I am not capable of otherwise. I mean that worship of Christ creates in me a vocational fire I do not have otherwise. I mean that prayer creates in me a prophetic rage toward the world's wretched injustices I cannot maintain otherwise. I have no clue whether or not I'm kinder or more generous than the average person, but I do know that I am kinder and more generous with Christ than I am without him.

And so if push came to shove, I would choose Christ over the truth because in a world without God, I would choose beauty over truth. In a world without God, the truth is vastly overrated. And if that causes you to puff out your chest in righteous indignation ("You're being a coward! Accept the truth!"), you are free to express that

sentiment—but frankly, I do not care. I have glimpsed the beauty of
the empty tomb, so even if it is a mirage, I'd be a fool to stop walking
toward it.

So what will it be: Christ or the truth? I think we can safely assume
we will never actually be forced to look down the barrel of Dostoyevsky's binary hypothetical, because there will be no irrefutably
"proving" Christ is or isn't the truth. Our decision is less severe: Given
that you have to choose and complete rational certitude isn't in the
cards, will you choose Christ or something else?

And so here is a case for faith in the worst case. If the fog of skepticism will not lift, and all the rational and theological and emotional
arguments leave you stuck in a place of exhausted paralysis, and you
have lost all faith that anything could happen to give you more faith,
walk toward Jesus. Why? Because he is beautiful. And even if the
worst case happens to be *the* case and Christianity is an untrue myth,
it's still a myth worth living—perhaps the only one. I can tell you
from experience the fog will lift, but even if it doesn't, walking toward
Jesus is really the only sane thing to do, and knowing that can be the
thing that keeps you from walking away. It was for me.

I still wish that small, smooth stone would inexplicably rattle
around in that old communion cup, but even if it does not, I will
stay with Christ. I cannot definitively prove Christ is the truth, but
I do know he is beautiful—so beautiful I would rather be wrong
about him than right about anything else.

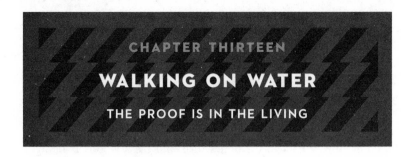

CHAPTER THIRTEEN

WALKING ON WATER

THE PROOF IS IN THE LIVING

*O*nce upon a time, a man walked on water.

On a stormy sea in the dead of night, twelve men huddled together. They cursed the wind and prayed prayers and gripped their tiny boat, and then, through the veil of driving rain, they saw a ghost. As the ghost came closer, their hearts beat faster, and while the record spares them the indignity of telling us what they cried out, it does tell us they cried out in fear. Twelve grown men were huddled together in a tiny boat, cursing and praying and yelling at a ghost. And then the ghost yelled back—

"Take courage! It's me! Don't be afraid."

I was fifteen the first time I imagined myself in that boat, and I've been imaging myself in it ever since. As my youth pastor told this story from Matthew 14, a sea bubbled up and the walls became the world all around; fluorescent lights, carpet squares, and white walls became menacing clouds, frothy waves, and an ashen horizon, and the thirty of us gripped the sides of our tiny boat.

What would I do? What would you do if the ghost yelled back? Never at a loss for words, Peter puts the ghost to the test—"Jesus, if that's really you, command me to come to you on the water."

"Come!"

"And Peter got out of the boat, and walked on the water" (Matthew 14:29).

Have you ever walked on water? Me neither. I wonder if the water felt flat and firm or heaving and unstable—was it like walking on a sidewalk or a waterbed? I'd guess the latter, and as Peter finds his sea legs, he has a moment of self-awareness and realizes he is doing something that cannot be done—he is walking on water. How is he walking on water? Did his bones turn into balsa wood? Is he light as a feather? Or did the water somehow solidify? Dense clusters of salt acting like stepping stones? We do not know, but we do know his flash of self-awareness breaks the spell, whatever magic is at work disappears, and Peter begins to sink. Peter sinks when he tries to explain a mystery instead of live it.

THE CHOREOGRAPHY OF FAITH

The saints tell us faith follows a journey from innocence to doubt to mystery. This movement is the grand arc of our lives and the plot of each day. Reason has short wings. The Bible alone is a poor remedy for doubt. Isolated rituals can deaden instead of enliven. I am not aware of a single incontestable, indisputable, knockdown, silver-bullet argument for the truthfulness of Christianity. But discipleship is the choreography of faith, and when Scripture, prayer, community, mission, reason, and ritual move in rhythm, I live the mystery and find myself walking on water. Many of us cannot point to a direct experience, but we cannot help but affirm that "present throughout [our] life as a whole, there is a total experience of the living God, a conviction existing on a level more fundamental than all [our] doubts."

God is not the mystery I understand but the mystery that seems to best understand all the mysteries in me. God does not make sense *to* me so much as God makes sense *of* me—my hopes and fears, dreams and reasonings, consistencies and contradictions, rapturous almsgivings and damning iniquities. When I step out on the waters and get *inside* faith, I do not sense certainty, but I do sense stability. Like Augustine, my desire is "not to be more certain about you, but to be more stable in you."

I also sink—a lot. I get so fixated on explaining the mystery that I forget to live it. Kallistos Ware reminds us that "it is not the task of Christianity to provide easy answers to every question, but to make us progressively aware of a mystery. God is not so much the object of our knowledge as the cause of our wonder."

A fantastical scene breaks out in Acts 2. The Holy Spirit falls like fire and a gang of illiterate Jews start chattering in languages they cannot speak. The gathered crowd realizes something atypical is happening but is split in its reaction to the oddity. Some jeer: "These poor peasants are inebriated on sweet wine!" Others wonder: "What does this mean?" Arrested by mystery, we must respond with cynicism or wonder.

Cynicism is easy, safe, indulgent, progressive, and most of all, boring. It shrinks the world down to manageable size—but the world is not manageable. I love being cynical for a whole host of reasons, but mostly because it helps me stay in control. In the remote corner of a Majority World country, I once had a seemingly sensible pastor tell me he had seen a man healed who had been paralyzed for twenty years, and I smiled and nodded and thought to myself how sad it must be for him to not be like me and know things like that don't happen. Then he introduced me to the man. Then he told me he reckoned half the Christians in his country were Christians because they or someone they knew had experienced some sort of physical healing. The cynic in me hemmed and hawed.

We respond with cynicism when we don't want to be duped; we respond with wonder when we don't want to miss out. We respond with cynicism because we desire control; we respond with wonder because we desire delight. I've always felt Robert Adams explains this better than anyone:

> From the standpoint of control . . . pessimism seems a stronger position than optimism. I think this fact is the main source of the intellectual machismo that prides itself on a sort of "tough-mindedness" that refuses to hope for very much. The desire for control tempts us to believe that if we hope for too much we will make fools of ourselves, whereas if we turn out to have hoped for too little we will only have proved to be "stronger" than we needed to be. This machismo is no more rational than the wishful thinking of which the hopeful are often accused. . . . Pessimism is not happier than optimism; hope is happier than despair. But it is quite possible to prefer control to happiness.
>
> What Christianity promises may seem "too good to be true"; the emotional meaning of this is that Christianity promises more than we can hope for without giving up control.

There are days when stepping out of bed is as courageous as crossing the Pacific on foot or flying to the moon with a bottle rocket taped to your back. We are all at the mercy of massive mysteries and should treat each other with great tenderness. So it is with great tenderness that I say realism is a terrible disease. I am a recovering realist. And in my recovery, I am learning that realism is an understandable but cowardly attempt to stay in control by refusing to hope. I am learning that the ludicrous dream of Christianity is supposed to seem too good to be true and that if I want to embrace it, I must give up control. There is no other way. It is too big and beautiful to hedge on. I am learning the opposite of cynicism is not naiveté, but wonder.

LIKE A CHILD

My little boy is growing up. His world is still enchanted, but the spell is breaking. Since I started this book, birds are no longer as miraculous as unicorns. I try not to get too sentimental about it all. Little boys aren't supposed to become Peter Pans; they are supposed to grow up. I do not want him to stay childish, but I do want him to stay childlike. I don't want him to "lose innocence and wonder; but to proceed on the appointed journey: that journey upon which it is certainly not better to travel hopefully than to arrive, though we must travel hopefully if we are to arrive."

Jesus said we have to become like children if we want to enter the kingdom of God. This is no small task. It takes prodigious discipline and maturity to stay childlike. It's a daring thing for a cynical heart to seek, but you will grow "up" into the civilized banality of adulthood if you don't seek it. It is also the end of all wisdom because wisdom, says David Bentley Hart, "is the recovery of innocence at the far end of experience."

Wisdom is a sort of second naiveté, returning to curiosity and turning from ambition, receiving all things as gifts instead of grasping them as possessions. Wisdom is not getting so obsessed explaining the mystery you forget to live it.

This is so because no matter how long we live or how much we learn, there will always be a gap between what we know and what we wish we knew. Much modern Christian apologetics has lost sight of this gap, resulting in a self-congratulatory culture wherein we take shortcuts, overstate ourselves, and make a case for faith that doesn't require faith so much as (allegedly) clear-eyed comprehension of (allegedly) indisputable historical and rational arguments. Moving past this approach requires accepting that we can reason ourselves *toward* faith but never all the way to faith. The gap remains. What will we do with it?

Søren Kierkegaard once reminded us that following Jesus requires a leap of faith, or perhaps more accurately, a leap to faith. He likens it to something called a tilting doll, a toy rounded on the bottom and weighted such that it will always right itself when pushed over. Faith, says Kierkegaard, is like that tilting doll. It will stand on its own, but the only way to "prove" it is to let it go so it can right itself: "As long as I keep my hold on the proof . . . the [proof of God's] existence does not come out, if for no other reason than that I am engaged in proving it; but when I let the proof go, the existence is there . . . the existence emerges . . . by a leap." In other words, the proof emerges in the leap that is a life of faith. The proof is always in the living.

A few days removed from a near fatal heart attack, famed Jewish theologian Abraham Joshua Heschel was visited by a dear friend, and Heschel confided that when he regained consciousness and realized he was alive, he did not feel anger, but gratitude—gratitude for every moment he had lived. And then he reiterated the prayerful request at the heart of his life's work: "I did not ask for success; I asked for wonder. And You gave it to me."

I cannot say with irrefutable certainty that God is real, that Jesus was resurrected, or that the world will end with the revelry of the kingdom of God. I am an amateur graffiti vandal. I am an ant on a rollercoaster. What I know will always be less than the great hope I feel.

I *can* say that when I experience the absence of God, I miss him terribly, and that experiencing the absence of God is "not just very different from, but incompatible with, treating that something or someone as nonexistent." I can say, "There is no tale ever told that men would rather find was true." I can say Jesus is beautiful. And I can say that I have walked out on the waters of faith and felt stability beneath my feet, so while I occasionally sink, that's much better than spending the rest of my life in the boat. Besides, every sinking can be a baptism, a deeper immersion into God's beautiful, terrible, but ultimately beautiful world.

I would love invincible certainty, but I don't ask for it anymore. Instead, I ask for wonder. Wonder keeps my senses sharp, my heart open, my spirit nimble. Wonder and faith need each other. When our inner cynic taunts the unbelievability of our faith, wonder reminds us that life *is* unbelievable.

In this secular age, we have fooled ourselves into thinking we understand much more of reality than we really do. We have fooled ourselves into thinking life is believable, is fundamentally explicable by evolution and equations. But this is sophisticated madness. Yes, we can send a man to the moon. Yes, we can map the human genome. No, we cannot explain the most basic of human mysteries—things like existence, consciousness, and love. So if we can behold the world, yawn, and say to ourselves, "Nothing out of the ordinary here," then we really should check our pulse, because we might be dead. We are miraculous creatures living in a miraculous world! It seems to follow that a miraculous faith is only reasonable. In other words, I ask for wonder because wonder keeps me realistic, in the proper sense of the term—soberly aware of things as they really are, miraculous and unbelievable.

The story of the universe hangs in a print of a painting on my wall—a man embraces his son and four people watch. I still see the woman in the shadows. I still spend time in the shadows with her— standing in the dark, looking at faith through sick glass, intrigued but also mystified and lost.

But my doubts don't scare me so much anymore, and I avoid chronically taking my spiritual temperature, worried those doubts will do me in. That's as counterproductive as digging up a plant each morning to see how its roots are doing. In this way, doubts are like children—they need our attention but not our total attention, lest they become impossibly self-aggrandizing and self-referential.

My doubts remain, but my faith is no longer stuck in the shadows. I have felt the hands of the Father on my tired, doubting shoulders as I've stood there. If those hands rest on my shoulders, even in the shadows, where could I ever go to escape them?

ACKNOWLEDGMENTS

No book is an island, and many people contributed many things to make this little book happen. My wife, Allison, is as sweet and affable a woman as you'll find. She's also smart as a whip and has no tolerance for cheap answers or theological twaddle. She makes the world a more honest place. Thanks for keeping me, and my theology, honest.

Thanks to my brother, Adam, for being my brother, best friend, and most trusted theological confidant.

Thanks to the Fischer/Tatum/Brown/Ghant clan.

Thanks to my other family, Vista Community Church. You're a brave and loving lot, and this book was birthed from our journey together.

Thanks to Nate Hansen for, once again, helping me write with a prose more worthier of the ideas it tries to explain. (I know you're so proud.)

Thanks to Joel Perritte for, once again, providing encouragement and (charitably) critical feedback. Everyone should have a Joel.

Thanks to Roger Olson for believing in me.

Thanks to InterVarsity Press (especially Anna Gissing and Ethan McCarthy) for believing in this book, leaving it better than you found it, and helping me send it out into the world.

DISCUSSION QUESTIONS

1 GRAFFITI

1. Have you been led to believe that your doubts disqualify you from having vibrant faith?
2. Why has the church led so many of us to believe we're not allowed to have doubts?
3. How could the apostles have actually seen the resurrected Christ and still doubted?
4. The church was built on the worshiping doubters that we know as the apostles. Does this encourage you as you deal with your doubts? Why or why not?

2 ANTS ON A ROLLERCOASTER

1. How can an increased awareness of the largeness and diversity of the world challenge our faith?
2. How can we best explain why we believe we can trust the Bible?
3. If, as finite humans, we cannot be 100 percent certain of anything, why would we think we could be 100 percent certain about our faith?
4. Have you ever caught yourself trying to convince yourself something is true? Why is that a strange way to think about faith?
5. Have you ever had an epistemological crisis? What was it like? What prompted it?

3 How to Survive a Hurricane

1. How does Job teach us to keep our faith, even while we wrestle with God?

2. Why might it be important to talk to God, even when we don't have anything nice to say?

3. How might telling the truth about our doubts be the first step toward being faithful with them?

4. What doubts do you need to tell the truth about?

4 Beautiful, Terrible World

1. Is there a correlation between our sensitivity to beauty and our sensitivity to suffering? If so, what is it?

2. Has there ever been a moment or season of life in which you were so grieved by the world's suffering that it made faith very difficult? Can you describe that experience?

3. Do you think we should be careful about how much reality we expose ourselves to? Why or why not?

4. In what sense can a crisis of faith caused by suffering actually be an expression of faith?

5. Do you think that, if there is no God, there could still be such a thing as evil? Why or why not?

5 Four-Letter Word

1. Which story do you think makes best sense of evil: the story of evil, sovereignty, and the glory of God, or the story of evil, freedom, and the love of God? Why did you choose that story?

2. If God could have produced a Bible that clearly answered all our questions and left no room for interpretation, why do you think God produced a Bible that doesn't clearly answer all our questions and thus requires our interpretation?

3. How do we strike the balance between surrendering to evil and rebelling against it?

6 SILENCE

1. Has there been a time when you asked God for some whisper or sign of his presence, but all you got was silence?
2. Why do we tend to obsess over why bad things happen but rarely wonder why good things happen?
3. Is it possible that God is often doing things in our lives, but we're blinded to seeing, sensing, and hearing them? Can you think of an example of something good God has done in your life that you've overlooked?
4. Have you ever had a prayer answered?

7 DEATH BY FUNDAMENTALISM

1. How have you been influenced by fundamentalism?
2. Does fundamentalism threaten Christian faith? If yes, how?
3. Do you think that reading the Bible faithfully means reading it as literally as possible? Why or why not?
4. Do you think it's important to try to read the Bible as the human writer intended? Why or why not?
5. What are some ways we can respond lovingly but firmly to fundamentalism?

8 SCIENCE

1. Do you see any potential conflicts between Christian faith and modern science? What are they?
2. Do you think it's a mistake to set up God and nature as competitors? To think that either God does something or nature does it?
3. Do you think we should read Genesis 1–2 literally? Why or why not? What does *literally* mean for you in this context?

4. If the current findings of science are true, and humans were not created instantly a few thousand years ago but gradually over hundreds of thousands of years, how does that affect your understanding of Christian faith?

5. What questions do you have about harmonizing the modern theory of evolution with the biblical account of creation?

9 STUFF

1. Do you think that you mostly *think* your way through the world, or mostly *want* your way through the world?

2. How might a desire for stuff cause us to lose our faith?

3. Why do you think that, generally speaking, the poor tend to be more religious than the rich?

10 HELL

1. Do you struggle with the idea of hell as eternal, conscious torment? Why or why not?

2. What do you think of the idea that the doors of hell are locked on the inside?

3. What do you think of the idea that hell is the love of God experienced as wrath by frostbitten souls filled with hate?

4. Does hell as self-annihilation make more sense to you than hell as eternal, conscious torment?

5. Do you think we should hope that everyone is saved? Why or why not?

11 FAITH, DOUBT, AND LOVE

1. Is faith a means to love, or an end in itself? Why did you give that answer?

2. In combating doubt, why might it be a mistake to aim exclusively at faith and neglect aiming at love?

3. Has love ever resulted in faith for you?

4. How might understanding faith as the presence of love instead of the absence of doubt change the way we pursue faith?

12 CHRIST OR THE TRUTH?

1. Is belief in God an "essentially contested belief"?
2. Perform this thought experiment: In a worst-case scenario, where you had to choose between Christ and the truth, what would you choose? Why?
3. Do you think you're kinder and more generous with Christ than you are without him? Why?

13 WALKING ON WATER

1. Is cynicism an attempt to stay in control by refusing to hope? Why or why not?
2. How might seeking wonder be a more appropriate response to doubt than seeking certainty?
3. How might we be honest about our doubts without becoming obsessed with them, and without constantly taking our spiritual temperature?
4. If discipleship is the choreography of faith wherein various elements like Scripture, prayer, theology, reason, and community work together to bring our faith to life, have you ever so focused on one element that you've neglected the bigger dance?

NOTES

1 GRAFFITI

5   *a moment stretching into eternity*: Horst Woldemar Janson and Anthony F. Janson, *History of Art: The Western Tradition*, 6th ed. (London: Pearson College Division, 2003), 598.

6   *A father's hand and a mother's*: Henri Nouwen, *The Return of the Prodigal Son* (New York: Image Books, 1994), 99.

     The return to the Father: Ibid., 123.

9   *Just as an athlete*: Stanley Hauerwas, *Approaching the End* (Grand Rapids: Eerdmans, 2013), 67.

10 *a third of people who leave faith*: Christian Smith with Melinda Lundquist Denton, *Soul Searching: The Religious and Spiritual Lives of American Teenagers* (New York: Oxford University Press, 2005), 89.

     cannot ask their most pressing questions: David Kinnaman, *You Lost Me* (Grand Rapids: Baker Books, 2011), 190.

     Christians are too confident: Ibid., 137.

11 *When they saw him*: Richard Edwards, "Uncertain Faith: Matthew's Portrait of the Disciples," in *Discipleship in the New Testament*, ed. Fernando F. Segovia (Minneapolis: Fortress, 1985), 59.

     The White Rose: "White Rose," Holocaust Encyclopedia (Washington, DC: United States Holocaust Museum), www.ushmm.org/wlc/en/article.php?ModuleId=10007188.

2 ANTS ON A ROLLERCOASTER

13 *Eta Carinae*: To be technical, it is a stellar system of two stars.

14 *We find that we live*: Carl Sagan, *Cosmos* (New York: Random House, 1980), 193.

14   *reasonable argument can be made*: David Kinnaman, *You Lost Me* (Grand Rapids: Baker Books, 2011), 38.

   we now create as much new information: Schmidt said this at the Techonomy conference in 2010. See MG Siegler, "Eric Schmidt: Every 2 Days We Create As Much Information As We Did Up To 2003," TechCrunch.com, August 4, 2010, techcrunch.com/2010/08/04 /schmidt-data/.

15   *Human life in the western world*: Brad Gregory, *The Unintended Reformation* (Cambridge, MA: Belknap Press, 2015), 11.

   I once listened to a podcast: Greg Boyd and Andrew Whyte, interview by Justin Brierley, *Unbelievable?*, podcast audio, April 26, 2014, www .premierchristianradio.com/shows/saturday/unbelievable/episodes /greg-boyd-andrew-whyte-discuss-doubt-and-faith.

18   *Solomon affirmed the First Law of Thermodynamics*: So says John Mac-Arthur, "You Can Trust the Bible," sermon transcript, May 30, 1988, www.gty.org/library/sermons-library/80-51/you-can-trust-the-bible.

   When you are questioned: N. T. Wright, *Paul and the Faithfulness of God* (Minneapolis: Fortress, 2013), 34.

20   *there's a proper firmness*: Alan Jacobs, *How to Think* (New York: Currency, 2017), 127.

   The second problem: Greg Boyd, *Benefit of the Doubt: Breaking the Idol of Certainty* (Grand Rapids: Baker, 2013), 23-38.

21   *Doubt is not a pleasant condition*: See, e.g., Quodid.com, quodid.com /quotes/7062/voltaire/doubt-is-not-a-pleasant-condition-but-certainty.

22   *epistemological crisis*: A phrase coined by Alistair McIntyre in *Whose Justice? Whose Rationality?* (Notre Dame: University of Notre Dame Press, 1988), 354-58.

3 HOW TO SURVIVE A HURRICANE

26   *Everything nailed down*: From a character in the film *Green Pastures*, directed by Wolfgang Petersen (1936, Burbank, CA: Warner Archive, 2013); based on the play *The Green Pastures* by Marc Connelly.

27   *Job's archaic name*: Carol Newsom, "Job," in *New Interpreter's Bible: A Commentary in Twelve Volumes* (Nashville: Abingdon, 1996), 4:345.

   at odds with itself: Bruce Zuckerman, *Job the Silent: A Study in Historical Counterpoint* (New York: Oxford University Press, 1991), 14.

29   *Job's response is sincere*: Gustavo Gutierrez, *On Job* (Maryknoll, NY: Orbis Books, 1987), 6.

30   *Job did not sin with his lips*: B. B. Bat. 16a. Available at the Sefaria Library, William Davidson Talmud, www.sefaria.org/Bava_Batra.16a?lang=bi.

32   *His friends' arguments*: Gutierrez, *On Job*, 29.

34   *God's approval evidently refers*: Gutierrez, *On Job*, 11.

35   *Those who believe*: Miguel de Unamuno, *The Tragic Sense of Life*, trans. J. E. Crawford (New York: Dover, 1954), 193.

      the real erupts: To lift a phrase from Slavoj Žižek, *Looking Awry* (Cambridge, MA: MIT Press), 15.

36   *If the truth is worth telling*: Frederick Buechner, *Telling the Truth* (New York: Harper & Row, 1977), 5.

4 BEAUTIFUL, TERRIBLE WORLD

38   *The stars are bright*: U2, "Iris," *Hold Me Close*, Island Records, 2014.

39   *Can you understand why a little creature*: Fyodor Dostoyevsky, *The Brothers Karamazov*, trans. Constance Garnett (New York: Signet Classics, 2007), 273-74.

42   *Creation's being is God's pleasure*: David Bentley Hart, *The Beauty of the Infinite* (Grand Rapids: Eerdmans, 2003), 252.

45   *Here is the world*: Frederick Buechner, *Wishful Thinking* (New York: HarperCollins, 1993), 39.

      Can we carry the burden: Henri Nouwen, *Reaching Out* (1975; repr., New York: Image Books, 1986), 55.

46   *Maybe we have to be tolerant*: Ibid., 57.

      Only a God: Stanley Cavell, quoted in Peter Dula, *Cavell, Companionship, and Christian Theology* (New York: Oxford University Press, 2011), 167.

47   *Here is the world*: Frederick Buechner, *Wishful Thinking* (New York: HarperCollins, 1993), 39.

      trial of God: The story comes from Elie Wiesel, as recounted by Robert McAfee Brown in the introduction to Wiesel, *The Trial of God* (New York: Shocken Books, 1995), vii.

48   *The more a person believes*: Jürgen Moltmann, *The Trinity and the Kingdom* (Minneapolis: Fortress, 1993), 49.

49 *My brothers, a time of testing*: Albert Camus, *The Plague*, Modern
    Library ed. (New York: Random House, 1948), 201-2.

    a measure of what theology: Hart, *Beauty of the Infinite*, 3.

50 *Behind me, I heard the same man*: Elie Wiesel, *Night*, 3rd ed., trans.
    Marion Wiesel (New York: Hill and Wang, 2006), 65.

51 *instead of explaining our suffering*: Nicholas Wolterstorff, *Lament for
    a Son* (Grand Rapids: Eerdmans, 1987), 81.

5 FOUR-LETTER WORD

52 *Ultimately, responding to the surd*: John Polkinghorne, *Exploring Reality*
    (New Haven, CT: Yale University Press, 2005), 146.

    It is not really a question: Jürgen Moltmann, *The Trinity and the
    Kingdom* (Minneapolis: Fortress, 1993), 49 (emphasis in the original).

53 *We believe that from the beginning*: C. Everett Koop and Elizabeth
    Koop, *Sometimes Mountains Move* (Wheaton, IL: Tyndale House,
    1979), 25, 68.

    The only thing that angered me: Nicholas Wolterstorff, *Lament for a
    Son* (Grand Rapids: Eerdmans, 1987), 66.

54 *waiting to be systematized*: This my friend Roger Olson helpfully
    pointed out to me.

    Scripture is not a jumbled puzzle: To borrow an illustration from
    Christian Smith in *The Bible Made Impossible* (Grand Rapids: Brazos,
    2012), 43-47.

    two big stories: Though to be sure, there are countless variations on
    these two big stories.

55 *without himself being implicated*: Paul Helm, *The Providence of God*
    (Downers Grove, IL: IVP Academic, 1994), 104.

    What is true of the history of Joseph: Charles Hodge, *Systematic The-
    ology* (1871; repr., Grand Rapids: Eerdmans, 1986), 1:544.

    Scripture repudiates the claim: Mark Talbot, "'All the Good That Is
    Ours in Christ': Seeing God's Gracious Hand in the Hurts Others
    Do to Us," in *Suffering and the Sovereignty of God*, ed. John Piper
    and Justin Taylor (Wheaton, IL: Crossway, 2006), 47.

56 *Could we improve this picture*: N. D. Wilson, *Notes from the Tilt-a-
    Whirl* (Nashville: Thomas Nelson, 2009), 85.

57   *The shadows exist in the painting*: Wilson, *Notes*, 110.

     as it is impossible for a person to be forgiven: Helm, *Providence of God*, 215.

     So evil is necessary: Jonathan Edwards, *The Works of Jonathan Edwards* (London: Paternoster-Row, 1839), 2:528.

     for his glory and our good: *Our* here means "the elect's."

58   *no problem of evil in the Bible*: Greg Boyd makes this case well in chapter 1 of *God at War* (Downers Grove, IL: IVP Academic, 1997). What follows is much indebted to his work there.

     The early Christians: Walter Wink, *Engaging the Powers* (Minneapolis: Fortress, 1992), 314.

59   *preceding the events in Eden*: Forgetting this often leads people to assume physical death and destruction literally began at the point of Adam's primal act of disobedience. Of course, this is flatly contradicted by the discoveries of modern science, which show that physical decay far antecedes the dawn of humanity.

     a sphere of created autonomy: David Bentley Hart, *The Doors of the Sea* (Grand Rapids: Eerdmans, 2011), 62-63.

62   *encounter of the finite*: Polkinghorne, *Exploring Reality*, 143.

     the necessary cost: Polkinghorne, *Exploring Reality*, 144.

     Any attempts to tease: Boyd, *God at War*, 285.

     Evil and suffering exist: N. Berdyaev, quoted in Jürgen Moltmann, *The Trinity and the Kingdom* (Minneapolis: Fortress, 2011), 47.

63   *At face value*: Kenton Sparks, *God's Word in Human Hands* (Grand Rapids: Baker Academic, 2008), 244.

     more like a polyphonic novel: Christopher Wright, *Old Testament Ethics for the People of God* (Downers Grove, IL: InterVarsity Press, 2004), 444.

64   *If it is from Christ*: Hart, *Doors of the Sea*, 86-87.

66   *ordaining the world be set ablaze*: Some think God ordained the fall after his decision to create (infralapsarianism as opposed to supra-lapsarianism) and think this makes a great moral difference. I am not one of those people.

67 *not merely one divine property*: Hans Urs Von Balthasar, *Love Alone Is Credible* (San Francisco: Ignatius Press, 2004), 59 (emphasis in original).

We might experience love as wrath: See in particular David Bentley Hart, *The Experience of God* (New Haven, CT: Yale University Press, 2013), 125-28. And once again, if God's nature is ultimately anything other than love, it becomes hard to see how creation is not necessary, at least from a Christian perspective.

68 *than the happy knowledge*: Hart, *Doors of the Sea*, 103-4.

I am grateful God: Through primary and secondary causes, hidden and revealed wills, compatibilism, or whatever other means.

69 *No one can answer*: Moltmann, *Trinity*, 49.

6 SILENCE

74 *I had long read about martyrdom*: Shusaku Endo, *Silence* (1969; repr., New York: Taplinger, 1980), 60.

74 *The martyrdom of the Japanese Christians*: Endo, *Silence*, 60-61.

75 *Darkness is such that I really do not see*: Mother Teresa, *Come Be My Light*, ed. Brian Kolodiejchuk (New York: Image Books, 2009), 210.

76 *to pay more attention*: Christena Cleveland, *Disunity in Christ* (Downers Grove, IL: InterVarsity Press, 2013), 134.

negative information weighs: T. A. Ito et al., "Negative Information Weighs More Heavily on the Brain: The Negativity Bias in Evaluative Categorizations," *Journal of Personality and Social Psychology* 75 (1998): 887.

82 *stand like a very small child*: Mother Teresa, *Come Be My Light*, 221.

7 DEATH BY FUNDAMENTALISM

85 *a view from nowhere*: A variation of the title of Thomas Nagel's masterful work *The View from Nowhere* (New York: Oxford University Press, 1986).

86 *intellectual disaster of fundamentalism*: To borrow a title from chapter 5 in Mark Noll, *The Scandal of the Evangelical Mind* (Grand Rapids: Eerdmans, 1995).

The Bible is to the theologian: Charles Hodge, *Systematic Theology* (1872–1873; repr., Grand Rapids: Eerdmans, 1952), 1:10-11.

86   *Southern Presbyterian Robert Breckenridge*: Robert Breckenridge, quoted in Noll, *Scandal*, 97.

     The Scriptures admit of being: Noll, *Scandal*, 98.

     careful, unbiased, systematic: R. A. Torrey, *What the Bible Teaches* (Chicago: Fleming H. Revell, 1898), 1.

     Systematic Theology is the collecting: Lewis Sperry Chafer, *Systematic Theology* (Dallas: Dallas Seminary Press, 1947), 1:x.

87   *it was often their weaker, more simplistic ideas*: Chafer, *Systematic Theology*, 1:57.

     one flattens out reality with the Bible: Or more precisely, Christian fundamentalism flattens out the actual Bible with a doctrine of the Bible.

88   *a significant minority of believers*: David Bentley Hart, *The Experience of God* (New Haven, CT: Yale University Press, 2013), 27.

91   *form of theological culture that assumes*: John Howard Yoder, *The War of the Lamb*, ed. Glen Stassen, Mark Thiessen Nation, and Matt Hamsher (Grand Rapids: Brazos, 2009), 34.

92   *And yet the version of Christianity that survived*: Noll, *Scandal*, 145.

     God did not choose to give us: Gordon Fee, "Hermeneutics and the Gender Debate," in *Discovering Biblical Equality: Complementarity Without Hierarchy*, ed. Ronald Pierce, Rebecca Groothuis, and Gordon Fee (Downers Grove, IL: InterVarsity Press, 2005), 370.

8 SCIENCE

94   *We should not lose our influence*: Something I heard Andy Stanley say at a Catalyst conference in April 2016.

95   *And surely all the crusading*: Michael Lipka, "10 Facts About Atheists," Pew Research Fact Tank, June 1, 2016, www.pewresearch.org/fact-tank /2016/06/01/10-facts-about-atheists/.

     Other faithful explorers: I especially recommend the work of John Polkinghorne, Alvin Plantinga, Keith Ward, and the BioLogos crew.

96   *Science takes things apart*: Jonathan Sacks, interview by Michael Schulson, "Jonathan Sacks on Richard Dawkins: 'New Atheists Lack a Sense of Humor,'" Salon.com, September 27, 2014, www.salon.com/2014/09/27 /jonathan_sacks_on_richard_dawkins_new_atheists_lack_a_sense _of_humor/.

97   *God is dead*: Friedrich Nietzsche, *The Gay Science*, ed. Walter Kaufmann (New York: Vintage, 1974), 181.

     ancient religions . . . axiological explanations: Keith Ward, *The Evidence for God* (London: Darton, Longman & Todd, 2014), 84.

98   *Every reputable survey*: For example, see any of the following: Larry Martz and Ann McDaniel, "Keeping God Out of Class (Washington and Bureau Reports)," *Newsweek*, June 29, 1987, 22-23; B. A. Robinson, "Results of Public Opinion Polls on Naturalistic Evolution, Theistic Evolution & Creation Science," ReligiousTolerance.org, last updated June 4, 2014, www.religioustolerance.org/ev_publi.htm; Pew Research Center, "Section 5: Evolution, Climate Change and Other Issues," in "Public Praises Science; Scientists Fault Public, Media," June 9, 2009, www.people-press.org/2009/07/09/section-5-evolution-climate -change-and-other-issues; Pew Research Center, "Chapter 3: Attitudes and Beliefs on Science and Technology Topics," in "Public and Scientists' Views on Science and Society" by Cary Funk and Lee Rainie, January 29, 2015, www.pewinternet.org/2015/01/29/chapter-3-attitudes -and-beliefs-on-science-and-technology-topics.

99   *The book is on the table*: Illustration borrowed from Brad Gregory, *The Unintended Reformation* (Cambridge, MA: Belknap Press, 2015), 33.

     To speak of "God" properly: David Bentley Hart, *The Experience of God* (New Haven, CT: Yale University Press, 2013), 30.

100 *fundamental doctrine of divine transcendence*: This theological creep, a combination of the metaphysical univocity of being and Occam's razor, is well documented by Gregory, *Unintended Reformation*, 25-73.

101 *when you run out of gaps*: Brian Zahnd tweeted this at some point.

     Everything is a miracle: Richard Taylor, *Metaphysics*, 4th ed. (Englewood Cliffs, NJ: Prentice Hall, 1992), 100-3.

102 *That there is a world*: Stanley Hauerwas, *Approaching the End* (Grand Rapids: Eerdmans, 2013), 10.

     In what specific ways does evolution: Alvin Plantinga proposes five or six, but I'm simplifying. *Where the Conflict Really Lies* (Oxford: Oxford University Press, 2011), 55.

103 *An overwhelmingly minority position*: James K. Smith references the "utter novelty of young-earth creationism" in his essay "From Culture

Wars to Common Witness," in *How I Changed My Mind About Evolution*, ed. Kathryn Applegate and J. B. Stump (Downers Grove, IL: IVP Academic, 2016), 25.

103   *Despite widespread impressions*: Mark Noll, *The Scandal of the Evangelical Mind* (Grand Rapids: Eerdmans, 1995), 188. For a further discussion, read Ronald Numbers's excellent book *The Creationists* (New York: Alfred A. Knopf, 1992).

Calvin's doctrine of creation: B. B. Warfield, "Calvin's Doctrine of Creation," *Princeton Theological Review* 13 (1915): 190-255, as quoted in *The Works of Benjamin B. Warfield*, vol. 5, *Calvin and Calvinism* (New York: Oxford University Press, 1931), 304-5.

104   *Augustine believed*: The same cannot be said for Luther, who was more rigid. He was also not the interpreter Augustine and Calvin were.

Augustine suggests that when science proves: Peter Harrison, "Is Science-Religion Conflict Always a Bad Thing?," in *Evolution and the Fall*, ed. William T. Cavanaugh and James K. A. Smith (Grand Rapids: Eerdmans, 2017), 211.

Darwinism casts us all down: P. R. Russel, "Darwinism Examined," *Advent Review and Sabbath Herald* 47 (1876): 153.

105   *when Christ took on human nature*: Ernan McMullin, quoted in Richard Mouw, "Safe Space," in Applegate and Stump, *How I Changed My Mind About Evolution*, 193.

106   *I think the word "intervention"*: Ward, *Evidence for God*, 39-40.

Some see problems: For example, Hart's suggestion (contra intelligent design) that the absence of a single instance of irreducible complexity is a more forceful argument in favor of God's rational action in creation than many instances of it. See *Experience of God*, 39.

acting specially in the world: Plantinga, *Where the Conflict*, 118.

107   *evolution makes us fundamentally revise*: The best current resource for sorting through issues attendant to this problem is Cavanaugh and Smith, *Evolution and the Fall*.

it appears we evolved: See Scot McKnight and Dennis R. Venema, *Adam and the Genome* (Grand Rapids: Brazos, 2017), particularly chapters 1-3.

107   *God created them unfinished*: I am borrowing from James K. A. Smith's succinct, imaginative explanation in Cavanaugh and Smith, *Evolution and the Fall*, 61-62.

108   *Eden in this model represents*: Celia Deane-Drummond, "In Adam All Die?," in Cavanaugh and Smith, *Evolution and the Fall*, 42.

      as Augustine reminded us: Harrison, "Is Science-Religion Conflict Always a Bad Thing?," 211.

109   *When you consider the millions*: Philip Kitcher, quoted in Plantinga, *Where the Conflict*, 57.

110   *the end is in the beginning*: Hauerwas, *Approaching the End*, 21.

112   *physics explains everything*: Hart, *Experience of God*, 77.

      It forgot the limits of scientific inquiry: Hart, *Experience of God*, 300.

      it is certain that all possible scientific findings: Gregory, *Unintended Reformation*, 71.

9 STUFF

114   *one of the seven princes of hell*: See, for example, Gregory of Nyssa, *The Lord's Prayer, The Beatitudes*, trans. Hilda Graef (New York: Paulist Press, 1954), 83.

115   *brains-on-a-stick*: To borrow a phrase from James K. A. Smith, *You Are What You Love* (Grand Rapids: Brazos, 2016), 3.

118   *1 Timothy 6:9-10*: Despite some complaints to the contrary, interpreting 1 Timothy 6:10 as "a root of all kinds of evil" is a mistaken attempt to soften the hyperbolic nature of this verse. See New English Translation's notes on 1 Timothy 6:10 for further clarification.

      If you want to build a ship: Antoine de Saint-Exupery, *The Wisdom of the Sands* (New York: Harcourt Brace, 1950), quoted in Smith, *You Are What You Love*, 11.

119   *a few foundational societal forces*: A story masterfully told by Brad Gregory in chapter 5 of *The Unintended Reformation*.

120   *amoral consumerama*: To borrow a phrase from James Twitchell, "Two Cheers for Materialism," in *The Consumer Society Reader*, ed. Juliet B. Schor and Douglas B. Holt (New York: Free Press, 2000), 282.

      Amid the hyperpluralism: Gregory, *Unintended Reformation*, 236.

121 *secularization is simply developed capitalism*: David Bentley Hart, "Mammon Ascendant," *First Things*, June/July 2016, 35.

Don't ask, don't tell: Smith, *You Are What You Love*, 53.

122 *most self-described atheists*: Michael Lipka, "10 Facts About Atheists," Pew Research Fact Tank, June 1, 2016, www.pewresearch.org/fact -tank/2016/06/01/10-facts-about-atheists/.

Religion is the sigh: Karl Marx, *Critique of Hegel's "Philosophy of Right,"* ed. Joseph O'Malley (Cambridge: Cambridge University Press, 1982), 131.

123 *Has Prometheus really been unbound*: See David Bentley Hart, *The Experience of God* (New Haven, CT: Yale University Press, 2013), 313.

10 HELL

127 *reconciled to God*: Frederick Dale Bruner, *The Gospel of John: A Commentary* (Grand Rapids: Eerdmans, 2012), 719.

128 *A place to undergo the fires*: Lewis tinkered with the idea that those in purgatory could either make their way to heaven or hell, and would subsequently find that they had been in either heaven or hell all along.

130 *What if death only forever*: Dallas Willard, *The Divine Conspiracy* (New York: HarperSanFrancisco, 1998), 302.

everything becomes more and more itself: C. S. Lewis, *The Great Divorce* (1946; repr., New York: HarperCollins, 2001), 132.

130 *You take that onion*: Fyodor Dostoyevsky, *The Brothers Karamazov*, trans. Constance Garnett (New York: Signet Classics, 2007), 405.

What we call hell: David Bentley Hart, *The Doors of the Sea* (Grand Rapids: Eerdmans, 2011), 85.

131 *the suffering of being unable*: Dostoyevsky, *Brothers Karamazov*, 371.

There will never be beings unloved: Gustave Martelet, *L'au-dela retrouve: Christologie des fins dernieres* (Desclee, 1974), quoted in Hans Urs Von Balthasar, *Dare We Hope "That All Men Be Saved"?* (San Francisco: Ignatius, 1988), 54.

If you think hell is: Tim Keller, "Questioning Christianity Session 4," www.livestream.com/redeemer-nyc/events/3938277/videos/82595164, accessed February 14, 2017.

132   *the doors of hell*: C. S. Lewis, *The Problem of Pain*, rev. ed. (New York: HarperOne, 2015), 130 (emphasis in original).

       Anyone who does not believe: Christian Gottlieb Barth, quoted in Jaroslav Pelikan, *The Melody of Theology: A Philosophical Dictionary* (Cambridge, MA: Harvard University Press, 1988), 5.

       just as God desires: For further reading, see Hans Urs Von Balthasar, *Dare We Hope "That All Men Be Saved"?*

       It may be: Lewis, *Great Divorce*, 140.

133   *I am thoroughly convinced*: Willard, *Divine Conspiracy*, 302.

       fires in heaven: Willard, *Divine Conspiracy*, 302.

       There is a great mystery here: N. T. Wright, *Surprised by Hope* (New York: HarperOne, 2008), 184.

       Stop arguing: Lesslie Newbigin, *Signs Amid the Rubble*, ed. Geoffrey Wainwright (Grand Rapids: Eerdmans, 2003), 120.

134   *not to let go of love*: Hans Urs Von Balthasar, *Love Alone Is Credible* (San Francisco: Ignatius Press, 2004), 94-96.

135   *It seems to me*: N. T. Wright, *Following Jesus* (Grand Rapids: Eerdmans, 2014), 95-96.

11 FAITH, DOUBT, AND LOVE

137   *Let me say*: Fyodor Dostoyevsky, *The Brothers Karamazov*, trans. Constance Garnett (New York: Signet Classics, 2007), 59-60.

141   *placing unprecedented emphasis*: Brad Gregory, *The Unintended Reformation* (Cambridge, MA: Belknap Press, 2015), 155.

       Promoted from its traditional subordination: Gregory, *Unintended Reformation*, 208.

142   *ordered primarily to the inconceivability*: Hans Urs Von Balthasar, *Love Alone Is Credible* (San Francisco: Ignatius Press, 2004), 101.

       The virtue of faith: Robert M. Adams has an excellent essay examining the question "What is virtuous about faith, *given that it is true*?" He explains it in terms of "relational goals." Robert M. Adams, "The Virtue of Faith," in *The Virtue of Faith* (New York: Oxford University Press, 1987), 20-23.

142   *Faith itself is the acceptance*: Alexander Schmemann, *For the Life of the World*, rev. ed. (Crestwood, NY: St. Vladimir's Seminary Press, 1973), 104-5.

143   *No doubt*: Dostoyevsky, *Brothers Karamazov*, 60.

145   *my inner atheist*: A term I learned in Daniel Taylor's delightful book *The Skeptical Believer* (St. Paul, MN: Bog Walk Press, 2013).

12 CHRIST OR THE TRUTH?

149   *an essentially contested belief*: This is term I am borrowing from Keith Ward, who got it from an idea articulated by the psychologist William James. Keith Ward, *The Evidence for God* (London: Darton Longman & Todd, 2014), 135.

150   *even with all the empirical evidence*: Ward, *Evidence for God*, 135.

      universe that we observe: Richard Dawkins, *River Out of Eden* (New York: Basic Books, 2001), 133.

151   *I want to say*: Fyodor Dostoyevsky, *Letters of Fyodor Dostoyevsky to His Family and Friends*, trans. Ethel Colburn Mayne (London: Forgotten Books, 2012), 67-68.

153   *Christianity . . . was the end*: Alexander Schmemann, *For the Life of the World*, rev. ed. (Crestwood, NY: St. Vladimir's Seminary Press, 1973), 54.

154   *When, therefore, Christianity departs*: David Bentley Hart, *Atheist Delusions: The Christian Revolution and its Fashionable Enemies* (Ann Arbor: Sheridan Books, 2009), 230-31.

155   *in a world without God*: As Hart wryly observes, the resolute love and pursuit of the truth is, inescapably, an affirmation of the reality of God, acknowledged or not. See David Bentley Hart, *The Experience of God* (New Haven, CT: Yale University Press, 2013), 250.

156   *I have glimpsed the beauty*: In a sense, I'm inverting Pascal's wager. Belief in God makes sense, not just because it allows you to avoid eternal perdition, but because it allows you to live a life of moral beauty.

13 WALKING ON WATER

158   *present throughout [our] life*: Kallistos Ware, *The Orthodox Way* (Crestwood, NY: St. Vladimir's Seminary Press, 1995), 18.

159   *not to be more certain*: Augustine, *Confessions* 8.i.1., quoted in Robert
      Louis Wilken, *The Spirit of Early Christian Thought* (New Haven, CT:
      Yale University Press, 2005), 311.

      it is not the task of Christianity: Ware, *Orthodox Way*, 14.

160   *From the standpoint*: Robert M. Adams, *The Virtue of Faith* (New
      York: Oxford University Press, 1987), 19.

161   *lose innocence and wonder*: J. R. R. Tolkien, *Tree and Leaf* (1964; repr.,
      New York: HarperCollins, 2001), 45.

      prodigious discipline and maturity: Something Madeleine L'Engle reminds
      us of in *Walking on Water* (New York: North Point Press, 2001), 74.

      is the recovery of innocence: David Bentley Hart, *The Experience of
      God* (New Haven, CT: Yale University Press, 2013), 10.

162   *As long as I keep my hold*: Søren Kierkegaard, "The Absolute Paradox,"
      in *Faith and Reason*, ed. Paul Helm (New York: Oxford University
      Press, 1999), 231.

      I did not ask for success: Story recounted in Abraham Joshua Heschel,
      I Asked for Wonder, ed. Samuel H. Dresner (New York: Crossroad,
      1983), 7.

      What I know will always be: See Gustavo Gutierrez, *On Job* (Maryknoll,
      NY: Orbis Books, 1987), xi.

      not just very different from: Alasdair Macintyre, *Edith Stein*, quoted
      in Daniel Taylor, *The Skeptical Believer*, (St. Paul, MN: Bog Walk
      Press), 76n.

      There is no tale ever told: Tolkien, *Tree and Leaf*, 72.

164   *digging up a plant each morning*: A metaphor lifted from Francis
      Spufford, *Unapologetic: Why, Despite Everything, Christianity Can Still
      Make Emotional Sense* (New York: Harper One, 2013), 206.